SOCIAL ENTREPRENEURSHIP IN SPORT

The social role of sport enterprises is being increasingly recognized at both local and global levels. Sport has the ability to influence community cohesion, physical and mental health, social inclusivity, and provides positive role models across society. More businesses in sport are incorporating these social aspects into their plans as a way of differentiating themselves from their competitors. This, in turn, has led to more social innovation in sport. Recently, there has been more emphasis on social entrepreneurship in sport due to the growing need to capture its societal impact. This book explores the non-profit role sport plays in society, and demonstrates how social enterprises can both address some of the negative social outcomes of sport and support businesses as they develop their social objectives. The over-arching aim of the book is to focus on how social entrepreneurship in sport is important in developing a better global society.

Vanessa Ratten is an Associate Professor of Entrepreneurship and Innovation in the Department of Management, La Trobe Business School at La Trobe University, Melbourne, Australia. She teaches entrepreneurial business planning, managing innovation in organizations and entrepreneurship. She has previously been on the business faculty of Duquesne University, the University of Queensland, Queensland University of Technology and Deakin University. She is an established researcher and author in the field of entrepreneurship and won a Vice Chancellors award for community engagement with innovation and entrepreneurship programs.

SOCIAL ENTREPRENEURSHIP IN SPORT

How Sport Can Deliver Social Well-being

Vanessa Ratten

Routledge
Taylor & Francis Group

LONDON AND NEW YORK

First published 2020
by Routledge
2 Park Square, Milton Park, Abingdon, Oxon OX14 4RN

and by Routledge
52 Vanderbilt Avenue, New York, NY 10017

Routledge is an imprint of the Taylor & Francis Group, an informa business

British Library Cataloguing-in-Publication Data
A catalogue record for this book is available from the British Library

Library of Congress Cataloging-in-Publication Data
Names: Ratten, Vanessa, author.
Title: Social entrepreneurship in sport : how sport can
deliver social wellbeing / Vanessa Ratten.
Description: Abingdon, Oxon ; New York, NY : Routledge, 2020. |
Includes bibliographical references and index. |
Identifiers: LCCN 2019033861 (print) |
LCCN 2019033862 (ebook) | ISBN 9780815351672 (hardback) |
ISBN 9780815351689 (paperback) | ISBN 9781351141048 (ebook)
Subjects: LCSH: Sports–Social aspects. | Sports administration–Social aspects. |
Social entrepreneurship. | Well-being–Social aspects.
Classification: LCC GV706.5 .R37 2020 (print) |
LCC GV706.5 (ebook) | DDC 306.4/83–dc23
LC record available at https://lccn.loc.gov/2019033861
LC ebook record available at https://lccn.loc.gov/2019033862

ISBN: 978-0-8153-5167-2 (hbk)
ISBN: 978-0-8153-5168-9 (pbk)
ISBN: 978-1-351-14104-8 (ebk)

Typeset in Bembo
by Newgen Publishing UK

CONTENTS

LIST OF TABLES

ALSO BY VANESSA RATTEN

Sole authored books

Ratten, V. (2017) Sports Innovation Management, Routledge, United Kingdom.

Ratten, V. (2017) Entrepreneurship and Innovation in Smart Cities, Routledge, United Kingdom.

Ratten, V. (2018) Frugal Innovation, Routledge, United Kingdom.

Ratten, V. (2018) Sport Entrepreneurship: Developing and Sustaining an Entrepreneurial Sports Culture, Springer, United Kingdom.

Ratten, V. (2019) Sports Technology and Innovation: Assessing Cultural and Social Factors, Palgrave, United Kingdom.

Sole edited books

Ratten, V. (2019) Entrepreneurship and the Community: A Multidisciplinary Perspective on Creativity, Social Challenges and Business, Springer, Heidelberg.

Ratten, V. (2019) Technological Progress, Inequality and Entrepreneurship: From Consumer Division to Human Centricity, Springer, Heidelberg.

Ratten, V. (2019) Sport Entrepreneurship and Public Policy: Building a New Approach to Policy Making for Sport, Springer, Heidelberg.

Co-edited books

Ratten, V., Jones, P., Braga, V. and Marques, C. S. (2019) Subsistence Entrepreneurship: The Role of Collaborative Innovation, Sustainability and Social Goals, Springer, Heidelberg.

Ratten, V., Jones, P., Braga, V. and Marques, C. S. (2019) Sustainable Entrepreneurship: The Role of Collaboration in the Global Economy, Springer, Heidelberg.

Ratten, V., Braga, V., Alvarez-Garcia, J. and Del Rio-Rama, M. (2019) Entrepreneurship, Innovation and Inequality: Exploring Territorial Dynamics and Development, Routledge, United Kingdom.

Ratten, V., Braga, V., Alvarez-Garcia, J. and Del Rio-Rama, M. (2019) Tourism Innovation: Technology, Sustainability and Creativity, Routledge, United Kingdom.

Tajeddini, T., Ratten, V. and Merkle, T. (2019) Tourism, Hospitality and Digital Transformation: Strategic Management Aspects, Routledge, United Kingdom.

Ratten, V. and Dana, L.-P. (2019) Diversity and Entrepreneurship, Routledge, United Kingdom.

Dana, L.-P. and Ratten, V. (2019) Societal Entrepreneurship and Competitiveness, Emerald, United Kingdom.

Ratten, V. and Jones, P. (2018) Transformational Entrepreneurship, Routledge, United Kingdom.

Ramadani, V., Dana, L. and Ratten, V. (2018) Informal Ethnic Entrepreneurship: Future Research Paradigms for Creating Innovative Business Activity, Springer, United Kingdom.

Ferreira, J., Fayolle, A., Raposo, M. and Ratten, V. (2018) Entrepreneurial Universities, Edward Elgar, United Kingdom.

Dana, L.-P., Ratten, V. and Honyenuga, B. (2018) African Entrepreneurship: Challenges and Opportunities for Doing Business, Palgrave, United Kingdom.

Ratten, V., Ramadani, V., Dana, L.-P., Hisrich, R. and Ferreira, J. (2017) Gender and Family Entrepreneurship, Routledge, United Kingdom.

Ratten, V., Braga, V. and Marques, C. (2017) Knowledge, Learning and Innovation: Research Insights into Cross-Sector Collaboration, Springer, United Kingdom.

Ratten, V., Ramadani, V. and Dana, L.-P. (2017) Women's Entrepreneurship and Family Business, Routledge, United Kingdom.

Ferreira, J., Dana, L-P. and Ratten, V. (2016) Knowledge Spillovers and Strategic Entrepreneurship, Routledge, United Kingdom.

Ratten, V. and Ferreira, J. (2016) Sport Entrepreneurship and Innovation, Routledge, United Kingdom.

Ramadani, V., Dana, L.-P., Gërguri-Rashiti, S. and Ratten, V. (2016) Entrepreneurship and Management in an Islamic Context, Springer, United Kingdom.

Dana, L., Han, M., Ratten, V. and Welpe, I. (2009) The Handbook of Research on Asian Entrepreneurship, Edward Elgar, United Kingdom.

Dana, L., Han, M., Ratten, V. and Welpe, I. (2008) Handbook of Research on European Entrepreneurship: Internationalisation of Small Businesses, Edward Elgar, United Kingdom.

ACKNOWLEDGMENTS

The role of social entrepreneurship in sport is a topic that I have been thinking about and researching for some time. When I was in Pittsburgh in 2008, the realization that there were few research studies specifically on sport entrepreneurship first came into my realm of thought. At the time there was the global financial crisis that changed fundamentally the financial markets and created turmoil in the world economy. During this year I was lucky to be living in Pittsburgh with my mum Kaye Ratten. At the same time that I was working in Pittsburgh I taught a class of MBA students about social entrepreneurship. As it was my first summer spent in the United States, I was still getting to know the culture and business community.

I taught social entrepreneurship nightly but also in intensive mode during the summer. During discussions with students but also delving into the social entrepreneurship field I kept thinking, where are the sport examples? As Pittsburgh is very much orientated around sport in terms of ice hockey, baseball and football, I kept seeing good examples of how social entrepreneurship applied to a sport context. Despite this practical significance in the research I could find few papers or case studies about social entrepreneurship in sport. So, in 2008, I first started to explore the nexus between sport and social entrepreneurship in more detail.

During this research exploration I wrote some articles for scientific journals which have been seminal in the development of sport entrepreneurship as a research field. However, nearly ten years later I still felt a burgeoning desire to contribute more to the fields of both sport entrepreneurship and social entrepreneurship. This led me to think that a book was needed specifically on the subject and that I could use my past knowledge and experience of this topic in this endeavor. So I started researching more into the role of social entrepreneurship in sport by collecting articles and information. This took a lot of time as there are so many practical examples of social entrepreneurship in sport that were waiting to be discovered. Whilst the writing of this book began some time ago, only recently has it come to fruition. For this, I thank the support of my family including my mum Kaye who, whilst not physically around, still has a great spiritual presence. I also thank my dad David for his endless chats and thoughts about my research, for which I am tremendously grateful. My brothers are a huge source of support and tell me to persevere even when I find it hard to progress. I thank my brothers Hamish and Stuart for their nurturing and support and also for their help in getting me to where I am today. Lastly, I thank my niece Sakura Ratten for her delightful spirit and the happiness she brings to our family. As she is only 1 year old I hope she will read this book in the future and be inspired by the way social entrepreneurship shines a light on the sports industry.

1

SOCIAL ENTREPRENEURSHIP IN SPORT

An introduction

Introduction

Research on social entrepreneurship experienced a significant growth in the last decade due to the recognition that entrepreneurship should have social goals (Austin et al., 2006). In conjunction with this trend has been more interest in sport business, yet linking sport to social entrepreneurship has been a slow process (Ratten, 2010). This has resulted in a gap between sport and social entrepreneurship research and practice, which needs to be filled particularly given sport's social role in the global society. For the purposes of this chapter, social entrepreneurship in sport is viewed as a subset of overall entrepreneurship but it differs due to its social mission and can include different types such as those related to business, education, health, recreation and sponsorship.

A definitional concern around social entrepreneurship in sport is understanding its meaning compared to other types of entrepreneurship (Ratten and Babiak, 2010). There is something recognizable about social entrepreneurship in the way financial objectives are melded into social projects (Kimbu and Ngoasong, 2016). In sport the real nature of social entrepreneurship is distinctive as it incorporates non-profit auspices. However, we have not yet gotten to the sociological nature of social entrepreneurship in sport (Ratten, 2010). There are literally dozens of examples of social entrepreneurship occurring in the sport realm that make interesting practical examples. These examples make the case that social entrepreneurship is valuable to sport but it needs to be considered from an opportunity or necessity perspective depending on the circumstances (Ratten, 2011). Opportunity entrepreneurs are defined as "individuals who are pulled into entrepreneurship as they seek to exploit a perceived opportunity" (Williams and Williams, 2014:35). Within sport this can result in social entrepreneurship being used as a way to leverage social contacts and business opportunities. Necessity entrepreneurs are considered as "individuals who are pushed into entrepreneurship because all other options are absent or unsatisfactory" (Williams and Williams, 2014: 35). In a sport context this results in sports organizations being made to start social enterprises due to the perceived reputation and financial effects.

Early social entrepreneurship research came from a variety of disciplines including sociology, anthropology and business management. This made the initial research on social entrepreneurship come from a non-profit and community perspective and saw it as an eclectic field. This was a seminal approach to taking in the wider context of entrepreneurship research that had previously emphasized the economic imperatives of entrepreneurship. Based on the interest in social entrepreneurship, traditional entrepreneurship research changed to take into account more diverse perspectives. As a result the social entrepreneurship field evolved and became an interesting area to study. Sport researchers were slower on the uptake of social entrepreneurship despite the recognition of its importance (Ratten and Babiak, 2010). This was due to many of the sport journals not considering social entrepreneurship to be within their area of inquiry. This limited view of sport isolated the field from other disciplines (Ratten and Ratten, 2011). This has changed recently with great progress made in sport social enterprises and many sports organizations, both amateur and professional, are using social entrepreneurship. Thus, the reality for the sports industry is that social entrepreneurship is already a popular topic but the research on this area has been less quick to evolve.

The purpose of this chapter is to examine the role of social entrepreneurship in sport. Increasingly non-profit motives such as social value and contributing to society are gaining prominence in sport literature. This is due to more emphasis on sport business and practice being about societal contributions. The definition and use of social entrepreneurship in sport will be discussed in this chapter as a way to understand the rationale and importance of the book.

Social nature of sport

The exact nature of sport in terms of being a product or service is debatable as it constantly changes depending on the context. A better way to conceptualize sport in a general sense is as a commodity. As Vamplew (2018:659) states "sport becomes a commodity when either consumers are willing to pay to play or watch it or if it has a potential value rather than merely a use one." This definition acknowledges that the definition of sport changes depending on an individual's perception about its place in society. Sport has commonly been linked to leisure activities as it is viewed as a recreational pursuit that is conducted for the purpose of enjoyment. Delpy (1998:24) concurs with this view, stating that "the word 'sport' is in fact, a derivative of 'disport' meaning to divert oneself." This reflects the feeling of sport being a fun activity and not work. Whilst this sentiment has changed in recent times as more people play sport for work reasons, there is still a belief that sport is a leisure activity. People are motivated to play sport for different reasons including for friendship, health and educational benefits. However, there are ancillary activities associated with sport meaning that people do not directly have to play sport but can watch or manage the process.

The different types of sport products include player, spectator and associated categories (Vamplew, 2018). Player products involve a set of rules and terms of engagement that govern how sport is consumed. Vamplew (2018:659) highlights how player products "can be divided into five subcategories comprising, games, equipment and costume, instruction and assistance, facilities and clubs." Sport is a game and its length depends on the participation of its players. Most games have a set of instructions that need to be followed. Games can be solitary or involve a group of participants. Usually organized sport games have a referee or umpire who checks that the game is being played properly and according to the rules, and typically most sport games involve physical activity but with the increase in computer games this has changed. Electronic games are gaining in popularity and act as a complementary product to physical games, although there are people who prefer just electronic games and are not interested in physical activity.

Equipment can range from the balls, racquets, or bats needed to play the sport to associated devices that increase performance. Increasingly, sport equipment is becoming more technologically advanced in terms of materials used and how it is manufactured. This is also seen in the real-time usage of video replays to aid decisions made by umpires in sport. Many sports though still have the same type of equipment that was used when the sport began and this has not changed much at all. This helps to create a better benchmark of current and past performance. Newer sports like skateboarding have become popular due to changing living conditions such as increased numbers of people living in the inner city. Costume involves the clothing needed to play a game and uniforms are worn by players as a way to signal the team they belong to but also for functional reasons. In sport there is a link between fashion and uniform that means the style of clothing constantly changes. This is evident in the length and style of sport clothing and the colors worn by players. In football the length of shorts has constantly changed and this is linked to fashion trends. Other sporting events, such as the tennis at Wimbledon, traditionally require players to wear white whilst the Australian Open tennis, the first event of the season, prides itself on allowing players to wear all colors, including fluorescent or unusual combinations.

Sports organizations face challenges in balancing social and business objectives. Based on the discussion in this chapter, there is a diverse range of ways that sports organizations can be involved in social entrepreneurship. This underpins the practical way social entrepreneurship needs to be managed in sport including for health, social responsibility and other reasons. Edwards and Rowe (2019:1) state "sport has become a popular policy tool for social outreach, intervention and prevention for all." Despite the view of sport being more aligned with business principles, there is still a need for sport to espouse social values (Suseno and Ratten, 2007). This is important as sport can be used as a social policy tool to help alleviate physical, mental and religious differences. Thus, the social consequences of sport and its related activities have an impact on society. As Delpy (1998:24) states "due to its universal appeal, sport is regarded as the world's largest social phenomenon." This means that sport, in terms of both direct and indirect activity, is one of the world's greatest social activities but, unlike other industry segments, it also has an emotional effect due to its entrepreneurial nature.

Social entrepreneurship

Social entrepreneurship has many different types of definitions that align with the topic of interest. Depending on the context, social entrepreneurship can be defined from a business, economics, engineering, science and technology perspective using either a narrow or a broad approach. The narrow approach defines it as involving entrepreneurial activities in the non-profit sector (Galera and Borzaga, 2009). This restricts entrepreneurial behavior in order to focus explicitly on those businesses with a social mission (Suseno and Ratten, 2007). Most non-profit organizations have social objectives but the magnitude differs depending on the size. Thus, it is essential to also consider a broad definition that relies on a mindset that combines profit and social goals. Generally, social entrepreneurship can be defined as "the recognition, evaluation and exploitation of opportunities stemming from the basic and long-standing needs of society" (Pathak and Muralidharan, 2017:3). This broad definition acknowledges that the opportunity recognition process is at the heart of social entrepreneurship but it differs from other types of entrepreneurship due to its societal effects. There are different kinds of social goals derived from social entrepreneurship including education and health initiatives. This helps make sport more impactful on society due to the way it bridges community and business concerns.

In order to help fill gaps in society, social entrepreneurship can be used as a form of value creation. This is due to social entrepreneurship involving the recognition of opportunities that have a social purpose but also provide a community benefit (Luke and Chu, 2013). Whilst the core premise of social entrepreneurship is the pursuit of business activities that involve social changing practices there also needs to be engagement with the community in order for change to occur. This change means that in the sport context, social entrepreneurship involves the notion of profit and non-profit goals in the attainment of a societal objective. The key difference between entrepreneurship and social entrepreneurship is in the emphasis on collective benefits rather than purely individual ones.

Social entrepreneurship involves two main activities, "instituting or increasing user fees, and … revenue augmentation through non-profit ventures – with the net effect in both cases to increase 'earned income'" (Zietlow, 2001:20). These activities affect the way social entrepreneurship applies in practice, being based on adopting then sustaining a social value through engaging in a business activity. The ability to recognize a social value may be based on having a heightened sense of social responsibility (Brickson, 2007). Thus, social entrepreneurs need to act boldly by continually learning about new innovations. This can be a relentless pursuit that depends on accessing the right kinds of resources (Brooker and Joppe, 2014).

There are two main typologies to understanding the role of social entrepreneurship in society–social orientation and socio-economic orientation (Goyal et al., 2016). The social orientation school of thought focuses on how social issues need to be addressed through change processes. This means highlighting the social impact of businesses by encouraging outreach activities. In order to implement social change there needs to be an evaluation of the cash flow that comes from philanthropic endeavors. This includes the beneficial arrangements that social organizations have that enable them to design better social projects. The second school of thought involves socio-economic change, which encapsulates the view that financial incentives are required to drive social value creation (Brickson, 2007). In this perspective, a sustainable business model is needed to change the way resources are used for social needs. This includes having specific metrics in place that enable an innovative value-driven approach to take shape (Brooker and Joppe, 2014). This may involve an element of risk as some of the metrics are designed to meet social needs.

There are numerous ways to conceptualize social entrepreneurship with no common approach existing in the literature (Galera and Borzaga, 2009). Most definitions tend to focus on behavior, sustainability, or market approaches. In the behavioral perspective, leadership plays a role in encouraging enterprises to become socially orientated. This is evident in Roberts and Woods (2005) who view social entrepreneurship as the pursuit of transformational social change that is conducted by visionary individuals. This sense of passion is seen in the way enterprises pursue opportunities that are socially orientated (Kimbu and Ngoasong, 2016). To do this organizations need to construct their behavior in a way that delivers social value through exploiting opportunities (Weerawardena and Mort, 2006). Thus, the perspective of social opportunities is evaluated through reconfiguring resources that can achieve social missions (Tracey and Phillips, 2007). Organizations, in order to be considered as socially constructed, need to often rely on government subsidies. The sustainability-focused definitions of social entrepreneurship highlight pro-social motives that assure long-term wealth generation. Thus, social outcomes are emphasized that involve accepting risks but pursuing value creation. To address social needs, organizations need to combine resources in new ways. This includes innovative use of resources to enable learning to occur. Khervieux et al. (2010) suggest that both economic and social considerations are required in social enterprises.

Santos (2012) proposed a positive theory of social entrepreneurship to highlight the need for value creation instead of value capture. This means that organizations should pursue sustainable solutions that can enable social improvement. Another approach to define social entrepreneurship is the market-based approach to social entrepreneurship, which stresses the need for social value to be created through market-based solutions (Alcantara and Kshetri, 2013). Thus, social entrepreneurship is a contemporary way to include a charity perspective within social problem-solving. This approach is complemented by Marshall (2011), who defines social entrepreneurship through the commercial exchange of goods or services that create social value. Thus, the discovery of opportunities needs to be based both on social need and the ability to do this in the marketplace through social ventures.

Social ventures

Embracing entrepreneurship and using social ventures as a business strategy has become popular amongst sports organizations. This especially occurs in amateur and community sports organizations where engagement with the local region is a survival strategy. Social ventures are defined as "an entrepreneurial form of organization that combines social, or public benefit aims with business-like management" (Margiono et al., 2017:1). The key differentiating factor between social ventures and other third sector organizations is that the individuals in the venture have a right to appropriate profits in a way they deem fit. This means the profits are often reinvested in other interests as a way to further maximize overall profits. Other third sector organizations include charities, credit unions and religious organizations (Seanor et al., 2013). These organizations normally do not distribute profits or are privately owned (Margiono et al., 2017).

Margiono et al. (2017) suggest there are four main characteristics of social ventures: (1) mission to create public/social value, (2) private ownership logic, (3) public or private funding and (4) public or private control. The first characteristic focuses on creating a form of public or social value that is different to purely financial value. Sports clubs are often seen as a key part of community and play an important role in capturing value. For local sports clubs, their social mission might be to instill a healthy lifestyle amongst participants through social engagement. Other sports clubs might be a result of local council initiatives that aim to increase active lifestyles. Thus, the social mission of sports clubs will differ depending on the type of sport played and the location. The social mission can be embedded in sport in a number of different ways, such as increasing the social impact of a sport to leverage resources in the community. The second characteristic involves private ownership logic. This means that the social venture is controlled by individuals and is not a separate unit of an organization. The third characteristic is public or private funding for social business activities. Public funding can be in the form of grants or tax incentives that help a social venture enter the marketplace. Private funding normally comes from a cause-related activity that is interested in tying their interests to the social venture. Characteristic four is private or public control, which determines how the social venture is run. Depending on the type of control, there will be different stakeholders who engage with the venture.

Social ventures enable strategic actions undertaken by sport entrepreneurs when using social entrepreneurship-based business models. This can help sports organizations target the more social needs of society through a process of symbiosis and correspondingly manage these challenges. Symbiosis is a way to consider alternative entrepreneurship strategies that are configured in different ways compared to typical market transactions. Dana et al. (2008:109) define symbiosis as "an approach that allows entrepreneurs and their firms to benefit from a multi-polar distribution of power and control." This is helpful in understanding social entrepreneurship in sport as it requires different kinds of power relationships in order to be effective. Sport entities are moving towards multi-powered network arrangements due to the variety of stakeholders involved in sport. As governments outsource sport programs, this power is divided amongst the entities who have the resources to implement social change. Symbiotic relationships in sport tend to include multiple partners that enable them to be social entrepreneurs. Even if one partner refrains from exercising their power, then other sport firms can develop relationships enabling the creation of more networks. This is happening in the online environment with sport users and organizations discovering interdependent relationships. This enables different people to benefit from the joint effort of all involved organizations.

Whilst there is an abundance of information on opportunity identification in the entrepreneurship literature, there is less on social opportunity identification (Gonzalez et al., 2017). Social ventures fill the gap in the process about the idea of using social opportunity recognition in a sports setting. In this way, I adapt the theory of social entrepreneurship to a sport setting by focusing on venture formation and this is important as there are few studies that have derived a new theory of social entrepreneurship in sport. Gonzalez et al. (2017:213) define social opportunity as "a potential business solution to address a social problem." Social opportunities help to shed light on social entrepreneurship in sport through the application of the theories of value creation and opportunity identification. Social value creation is defined as "resolving social issues such as generating income for the economically disadvantaged" (Corner and Ho, 2010). Social entrepreneurship includes social value creation considerations that have a social impact. This comes from entrepreneurship typically being considered as a way to create personal or shareholder wealth. The sheer size of the sports industry with the large number of small and amateur organizations makes it a specifically useful context for entrepreneurship. Whilst the literature on sport entrepreneurship is gaining momentum, the sub-topic of social entrepreneurship in sport is also gaining traction. This is due to the practice of social entrepreneurship in sport seeming to be ahead of research and theoretical development, which can be attributed to more research on sport focusing on organizational attributes such as strategy practices rather than entrepreneurial activity.

The strategy as a practice literature focuses on the actions of individuals rather than just organizations (Dahl et al., 2016). Individuals plan and act accordingly depending on changes in their environment and this is important in a sport context. Some situations need individuals to behave in certain ways in order to maintain their competitive advantage in the sport market. Other kinds of situations may involve individuals changing their behavior based on certain risk events. Risk-taking is defined as "the uncertainty that results from innovative behaviour" (Covin et al., 2016:5622). The level and nature of risk needs to be assessed in social entrepreneurship, particularly when sports organizations are involved in new social ventures.

The level of social salience in a sport organization will impact the kind of entrepreneurial activities in which they engage. Lortie et al. (2016:3) define social salience as "the importance entrepreneurs place on the social outcomes of their organisation." For amateur types of sports organizations, the social outcomes are likely to be more community- and civic-minded. For larger sports organizations the social outcomes might be to increase awareness about a specific health issue. Thus, the type of social outcome evident in the workings of a sports organization is likely to be tied to their size and context. In addition, specific social outcomes might be related to policy initiatives. More practical importance is being centered on the way sports organizations act entrepreneurially and have social outcomes, which is due to the internationalization and increased technological emphasis in sport. In addition, there is an increasing awareness about whether sports organizations are more entrepreneurial and civic-minded than other types of organizations. This comes from the perception that sport is viewed by many as entrepreneurial due to the new types of marketing and products it produces. However, some take a different approach, viewing sport as slow to change due to institutional inertia. Thus, social entrepreneurship in sport needs to be viewed in different ways depending on the social issue and level of entrepreneurship.

A sports organization is identified by the majority of their activities being around health or leisure pursuits and in order to be competitive they need to focus on new business ventures by being proactive. The process of proactiveness is defined as "efforts to take initiative, anticipating and enacting new opportunities, and creating or participating in emerging markets" (Covin et al., 2016:5621). Sports fans and stakeholders should play an active role in social entrepreneurship as they can identify new ideas and help promote the endeavor. More active sports fans are likely to engage more in social entrepreneurship programs as they can see emotional benefits stemming from their interaction. Thus, the responsiveness of sports fans to social entrepreneurship programs will vary considering the type of social issue or cause.

Aim of this book

The chapters in this book will show that sports organizations are often considered to be motivated by social entrepreneurship. The idea of this book is to build momentum on research into social entrepreneurship that takes a sports perspective. The growing consensus in sports studies is that an entrepreneurship approach is needed due to the dynamic nature of the sports industry, which has made the emerging research and practice on sport and social entrepreneurship take an interdisciplinary orientation. This enables new and creative research to evolve that builds on the research field of sport and social entrepreneurship. This book will cement the field of sport and social entrepreneurship as an innovative field that can lead to more meaningful research.

The chapters in this book will uncover new understandings about sport through portraying it as an area of importance for social entrepreneurship. To enhance our understanding of how sport is progressing, there needs to be an entrepreneurship perspective embedded in studies. In the past, entrepreneurship research in sport was largely ignored, which is surprising given the creative nature of many sports enterprises. Thus, an ongoing challenge for sport research is to develop newer theories, which is why social entrepreneurship research is so important. I believe that social entrepreneurship has many benefits to sport but can be a challenge to integrate into practice. In order to inform sports organizations about new developments social entrepreneurship can be used. This book will discuss how sport researchers need to be brave and embark on studies that utilize social entrepreneurship.

The theoretical development of this book is to question the prevailing theories about sports management to instill a social entrepreneurship approach. Using existing social entrepreneurship research applied to the sport context seems to be a valid way for examining this new field. However, as the chapters in this book will discuss, it is misleading to only use the existing social entrepreneurship research without considering the unique context of sport. The sports industry has different characteristics compared to other industries that need to be considered when asserting a social entrepreneurial perspective. The circumstances surrounding the sports organization, enterprise or individual for using social entrepreneurship needs to be analyzed. This means understanding the underlying nature of the sports-related social enterprise and how it is a product of the social and economic conditions. Therefore, there is a need to transcend current conceptualizations about social entrepreneurship in sport.

This book complements social entrepreneurship research that is extending the entrepreneurship debate in new directions. Existing research on social entrepreneurship has focused on diversity in terms of different types of social entrepreneurs but has not considered fully the industry context. This book will provide a detailed examination of social entrepreneurship opportunities in sport and ones that can be exploited. This will serve as a pathway to more research on social entrepreneurship value creation in sport and uncover new ways sport and social entrepreneurship can be combined.

More research is needed to understand how social entrepreneurship can be integrated into sport research. Sport is a vehicle for social progress and has many societal benefits. Sports organizations that pursue social entrepreneurship can contribute to poverty alleviation and sustainable development. Although the role of social entrepreneurship in sport has attracted attention, there is still a dearth of research on the topic. This book explores the following two research questions:

1. How can sport utilize social entrepreneurship?
2. How do sports organizations, athletes, managers and policymakers participate in social entrepreneurship?

The timing of having a book devoted to social entrepreneurship in sport is apposite to increased interest in the field. Social entrepreneurship is a relatively new field that will continue to grow with new ideas. The task of this book is to examine the potential patterns of social entrepreneurship in sports research for the future and adopts the position that a solid theory is needed in order to progress the field. The research on social entrepreneurship in sport needs to include the experiences of other disciplines in order to better understand the future nature of the field. Social entrepreneurship research already has a history of being a new field that gained acceptance but this book takes the next step by focusing on changes in sport made apparent by technology and social issues that have become intertwined with entrepreneurship research.

Sports theory implications

There is a sense of curiosity amongst sports researchers about how to integrate social entrepreneurship. This is due to many sports researchers feeling obliged to continue using existing theoretical paradigms and not include new theories. This sense of path dependency has been a deterrent to new topics like social entrepreneurship being used in sport. However, it is the intention of interdisciplinary research to use cutting edge theories from other fields in new contexts. I believe that social entrepreneurship can provide sports researchers with a supportive and contemporary theoretical background. It is reasonable to assume that emerging sports research utilizes social entrepreneurship in a challenging way. I am confident that social entrepreneurship will play a crucial role in the evolution of sport research.

This book is motivated by a lack of understanding about social entrepreneurship in sports literature. Until now, there have been few studies of social entrepreneurship in sport. The term "social entrepreneurship in sport" can signify any type of business activity in sport that has both economic and social goals. Social entrepreneurship can include both incremental and radical changes in sport. A more holistic framework to understanding social entrepreneurship in sport is required to delineate its characteristics. In this book, I acknowledge the critical role social entrepreneurs play in sport that is a result of their emphasis on social value creation. This book will shed light on the topic of social entrepreneurship in sport to provide a multi-level typology specific to sport. This will enable sport researchers to refine social entrepreneurship to enable the topic to be explored both individually but also contextually.

Sport research implications

Experiences learnt from the general literature on social entrepreneurship can be instructive to what can happen in sport and social entrepreneurship studies. The field of social entrepreneurship has changed over the past ten years with more people writing about the topic and more collaboration occurring. Sport and social entrepreneurship is a new era of social entrepreneurship research that is a unique field of study. This book has numerous policy implications for sport that help inform existing practices and improve new ones. There is little clarity about what the term social entrepreneurship in sport means and how it differs to other forms of entrepreneurship. Social entrepreneurship occurs in many industries but in a sport context it is made more noticeable by the number of amateur and community sports organizations that are in existence. This book will expand our thinking and knowledge about social entrepreneurship in sport, hereby opening new doors and ways to incorporate more social entrepreneurship research in sport.

The presence of social entrepreneurship in sport has been neglected so this book responds to the call for more research in this area. The effect of social entrepreneurship in sport operates through a system of network entities, which are embedded in the community. This book discusses how the sports industry is influenced by the social environment and provides suggestions about how to help social economic development. To do this, more social entrepreneurship dimensions are incorporated into the sport science debate. To proceed with this book, I commence by providing a framework for addressing the link between social entrepreneurship and sport. An overview of different facets of social entrepreneurship theory is then presented. More specific aspects and ideas about the nature of social entrepreneurship in sport are then presented. This helps to contribute to the research and policy implications for social entrepreneurship in a sport setting.

Social entrepreneurship in sport presents many opportunities but also challenges. On the positive side it will bring new ways of thinking about how sport engages with the community. This will enhance collaborative opportunities particularly those taking an interdisciplinary perspective. It will also unlock new patterns and relationships that were previously understudied in the literature. These opportunities will enlarge the literature on social entrepreneurship in sport but need to be balanced with the risks involved, which include placing too much emphasis on the social entrepreneurship literature without considering the unique aspects of the sports industry. Thus, a more thoughtful approach to research on social entrepreneurship in sport is needed, which takes into consideration the unique context of sport. The net result will be more research that encapsulates the importance of social change in sport but from an entrepreneurship perspective. The research on sport and social entrepreneurship will continue to achieve a long burst of productivity and will revolutionize the sport management field. It is an exciting time to do research on sport and social entrepreneurship as it meshes two disparate fields and will bring findings that will ultimately inform practice.

Sport management implications

There are a number of practical implications for sport managers involved in or considering social entrepreneurship. One of the most important considerations for sport managers is the time and cost of social entrepreneurship to their organization. For social entrepreneurs, sport is a good context to bridge the for-profit and non-profit worlds. Many sports organizations are the recipients of government funding so incorporating social entrepreneurship seems a logical step. More entrepreneurs need to use sport as a way to engage in social entrepreneurship. This includes negotiating and selecting different charities or social issues on which to focus. The sport sector is often an engine for innovation and growth so social entrepreneurs will be able to find a home for their activity. The results of this book suggest that entrepreneurs can aid social development by focusing on the sport sector.

For sport managers, the integration of social entrepreneurship into practice provides a new way of understanding sport. Whilst previous research on sport has tended to incorporate theories from other disciplines, a new theory of social entrepreneurship in sport provides a promising avenue for sport managers to integrate new practices into their organizations. New sport practices that include social entrepreneurship should further strengthen the field of social entrepreneurship in sport by exploring other factors that could be relevant. In addition, the testing of relationships between social entrepreneurship and sport performance is required in order to assess its relevance. This can make the practice of social entrepreneurship in sport more engaging and provide synergistic opportunities with other disciplines.

Conclusion

This introductory chapter of the book has focused on the reasons why a specific book on social entrepreneurship in sport is needed. Whilst there is an abundance of books on entrepreneurship and social entrepreneurship, there are none that stress the relevance of the sports industry. This book paves the way for a new industry context to emerge that is particularly relevant for social entrepreneurship practitioners and scholars. Social entrepreneurship in sport is an important topic area that will continue to grow in the future as more individuals, organizations and policymakers become aware of its potential. The definition and reason for social entrepreneurship in society was discussed in this chapter as a way of understanding its significance to the sports industry. The next chapters in the book will further discuss social entrepreneurship in sport by focusing on specific aspects that are important in today's globally competitive and technologically progressive marketplace.

References

Alcantara, L. L. and Kshetri, N. (2013) "The link between societal motivation and new venture performance: Evidence from entrepreneurs in Japan," *Journal of Small Business & Entrepreneurship*, 26(6): 623–641.

Austin, J., Stevenson, H. and Wei-Skillern, J. (2006) "Social and commercial entrepreneurship: Same, different or both?" *Entrepreneurship Theory and Practice*, 30(1): 1–22.

Brickson, S. (2007) "Organizational identity orientation: The genesis of the role of the firm and distinct forms of social value," *Academy of Management Review*, 32(3): 864–888.

Brooker, E. and Joppe, M. (2014) "Developing a tourism innovation typology: Leveraging liminal insights," *Journal of Travel Research*, 53(4): 500–508.

Corner, P. and Ho, M. (2010) "How opportunities develop in social entrepreneurship," *Entrepreneurship Theory and Practice*, 34(4): 635–659.

Covin, J. G., Eggers, F., Kraus, S., Cheng, C. and Chang, M. (2016) "Marketing related resources and radical innovativeness in family and non-family firms: A configurational approach," *Journal of Business Research*, 69: 5620–5627.

Dahl, J., Kock, S. and Lundgren-Henriksson, E. (2016) "Conceptualizing coopetition strategy as practice: A multilevel interpretative framework," *International Studies of Management & Organization*, 46: 94–109.

Dana, L., Etemad, H. and Wright, R. (2008) "Toward a paradigm of symbiotic entrepreneurship," *International Journal of Entrepreneurship and Small Business*, 5(2): 109–126.

Delpy, L. (1998) "An overview of sport tourism: Building towards a dimensional framework," *Journal of Vacation Marketing*, 4(1): 23–38.

Edwards, M. B. and Rowe, K. (2019) "Managing sport for health: An introduction to the special issue," *Sport Management Review*, 22(1): 1–4.

Galera, G. and Borzaga, C. (2009) "Social enterprise: An international overview of its conceptual evolution and legal implementation," *Social Enterprise Journal*, 5(3): 210–228.

Gonzalez, M., Husted, B. and Aigner, D. (2017) "Opportunity discovery and creation in social entrepreneurship: An exploratory study in Mexico," *Journal of Business Research*, 81: 212–220.

Goyal, S., Sergi, B. and Jaiswal, M. (2016) "Understanding the challenges and strategic actions of social entrepreneurship at base of the pyramid," *Management Decision*, 54(2): 418–440.

Khervieux, C., Gedajlovic, E. and Turcotte, M. F. B. (2010) "The legitimization of social entrepreneurship," *Journal of Enterprising Communities: People and Places in the Global Economy*, 4(1): 37–67.

Kimbu, A. and Ngoasong, M. (2016) "Women as vectors of social entrepreneurship," *Annals of Tourism Research*, 60: 63–79.

Lortie, J., Castrogiovanni, G. and Lox, K. (2017) "Gender, social salience and social performance: How women pursue and perform in social ventures," *Entrepreneurship & Regional Development*, 29(1–2): 155–173.

Luke, B. and Chu, V. (2013) "Social enterprise versus social entrepreneurship: An examination of the 'why' and 'how' in pursuing social change," *International Small Business Journal*, 31(7): 764–784.

Margiono, A., Zolin, R. and Chang, A. (2018) "A typology of social venture business model configurations," *International Journal of Entrepreneurial Behavior & Research*, 24(3): 626–650.

Marshall, R. S. (2011) "Conceptualizing the international for-profit social entrepreneur," *Journal of Business Ethics*, 98(2): 183–198.

Pathak, S. and Muralidharan, E. (2017) "Economic inequality and social entrepreneurship," *Business & Society*, 1–41.

Ratten, V. (2010) "The future of sports management: A social responsibility, philanthropy and entrepreneurship perspective," *Journal of Management & Organization*, 16(4): 488–494.

Ratten, V. (2011) "Sport-based entrepreneurship: Towards a new theory of entrepreneurship and sport management," *International Entrepreneurship and Management Journal*, 7(1): 57–69.

Ratten, V. and Babiak, K. (2010) "The role of social responsibility, philanthropy and entrepreneurship in the sport industry," *Journal of Management & Organization*, 16(4): 482–487.

Ratten, V. and Ratten, H. (2011) "International sport marketing: Practical and future research implications," *Journal of Business & Industrial Marketing*, 26(8): 614–620.

Roberts, D. and Woods, C. (2005) "Changing the world on a shoestring: The concept of social entrepreneurship," *University of Auckland Business Review*, 7(1): 45–51.

Santos, F. M. (2012) "A positive theory of social entrepreneurship," *Journal of Business Ethics*, 111(3): 335–351.

Seanor, P., Bull, M., Baines, S. and Ridley-Duff, R. (2013) "Narratives of transition from social to enterprise: You can't get there from here," *International Journal of Entrepreneurial Behaviour & Research*, 19(3): 324–343.

Suseno, Y. and Ratten, V. (2007) "A theoretical framework of alliance performance: The role of trust, social capital and knowledge development," *Journal of Management & Organization*, 13(1): 4–23.

Tracey, P. and Phillips, N. (2007) "The distinctive challenge of educating social entrepreneurs: A postscript and rejoinder to the special issue on entrepreneurship education," *Academy of Management Learning & Education*, 6(2): 264–271.

Vamplew, W. (2018) "The commodification of sport: Exploring the nature of the sports product," *The International Journal of the History of Sport*, 35(7–8): 659–672.

Weerawardena, J. and Mort, G. S. (2006) "Investigating social entrepreneurship: A multidimensional model," *Journal of World Business*, 41(1): 21–35.

Williams, N. and Williams, C. (2014) "Beyond necessity versus opportunity entrepreneurship: Some lessons from English deprived urban neighbourhoods," *International Entrepreneurship and Management Journal*, 10: 23–40.

Zietlow, J. T. (2001) "Social entrepreneurship: Managerial, finance and marketing aspects," *Journal of Nonprofit & Public Sector Marketing*, 9(1–2): 19–43.

2
VALUE CREATION AND SOCIAL ENTREPRENEURSHIP

Introduction

To enhance the international competitiveness of the sports industry it must embrace entrepreneurship (Ratten and Jones, 2018). Sport is a uniting force for communities as it helps to develop social cohesion but also enable the experimentation of new innovations. Unlike other industries that require a lengthy process to introduce new technology, the sports industry has been a testing ground for innovation (Ratten, 2019). Athletes, fans and sports clubs have co-created the use of innovation both for personal but also for community needs. This has facilitated the pursuit of sporting excellence as the way sport is played and viewed has improved. The sports industry has long out-performed other industries in terms of introducing new innovations. In conjunction with this competitiveness has been the internationalization of sport made possible by the Internet and other technology (Ferreira et al., 2016). This has made the sports industry more crowded in terms of competition, which has impacted sport policy.

Governments at the local, regional, national and international levels have an important role to play in ensuring an entrepreneurial approach to policy is used (Ratten et al., 2016). Sports organizations need to reinforce entrepreneurial policy initiatives by encouraging innovation, risk-taking and creativity. This is important as athletes and sports clubs are viewed by role models in communities and have the capacity to affect other areas of society. Promoting an entrepreneurial stance in sport policy will send the message that the sports industry is one of the most creative industries. In order to implement a consistent message, sports organizations need to work with government authorities to encourage entrepreneurship. This can be in the form of entrepreneurial sport policy initiatives such as social inclusion, technology integration or knowledge dissemination. Expanding the role of entrepreneurship in sport will strengthen the ability of governments to make good policy directions.

Many studies on social entrepreneurship provide no theoretical explanations about the role of industry context (Anderson et al., 2019). Whilst it is difficult to explain how social entrepreneurship works in the sports industry, it is nonetheless worth the effort. This is due to the way the sports industry connects with the social sector in a way other industries do not. Unlike the manufacturing industry, the sports industry has a unique contextual focus that embeds a social component amongst many of its activities. Through its competitiveness, the sports industry is a hotbed of entrepreneurial activity. This is seen in the new technology products and services being used in sport. Whilst technological forms of sport entrepreneurship are evident there has been less emphasis on social entrepreneurship. This can partly be explained by the large role that volunteers and non-profit management have played in sport. A new way of viewing entrepreneurship is by taking a social entrepreneurship approach that is cognizant of non-profit motives but still has a business component.

Sports organizations on the whole implement more social policies than non-sports organizations. According to public sentiment, sports organizations have a responsibility to act in a social manner. Social entrepreneurship offers a way for sports organizations to instill a social spirit but also accomplish financial objectives, thereby positively affecting a sports organization's reputation but also encouraging creativity and innovation. To succeed in implementing social entrepreneurship policies there needs to be consistent support from senior management. A common theme in the literature about sports organizations is their distinctiveness compared to other organizations. Sports organizations engage with the community on social issues in a way that helps build their social identity. At the same time, some sports organizations have been criticized in terms of the nature and extent of their social commitments. This can be based on insufficient recognition of the social work they do in their wider community. The literature on sports organizations stretches back over 20 years and is mostly published in sport-specific journals. Whilst having a considerable lineage, the literature on sports organizations and social entrepreneurship has been slower in progressing. It is now recognized that there is a considerable amount of social entrepreneurship conducted by sports organizations.

Sports organizations have a high level of social capital due to their interactions with others in the community. This enables them to have a competitive and entrepreneurial advantage in the marketplace that is superior to other types of organizations. The main ways stakeholders help social enterprises to implement social innovation are by developing knowledge and building expertise and skills. Social entrepreneurship involves using market-based methods to solve social problems. Whilst social entrepreneurship research is prevalent in sociology, ethics and management research, it is less understood in the sport discipline. There is an implicit ethics foundation of most social entrepreneurship research as it promotes good behavior in society. This is evident in the utilitarian ethical reasoning of social entrepreneurship in terms of societal good. The discourse used by social entrepreneurs refers to the idea of doing good by helping society. Thus, the overarching sense of reason is in having a high moral ground in the practice of social entrepreneurship.

Irrespective of the type of social entrepreneurship, it will involve socially responsible business practices. The main idea for social entrepreneurs is to help the planet by creating social value. Thereby, social entrepreneurs receive moral approval through their actions. Social entrepreneurs tend to have personal qualities of empathy and integrity that distinguish their business practices from commercial ones. These characteristics are based on their emphasis on honesty as a guiding business principle. Altruistic reasons are central to the idea of social entrepreneurship but there can also be personal ones such as interest in a particular social cause, although there is a tendency to focus on altruistic reasons such as equality and tolerance in social entrepreneurship. This reflects a need to achieve a sense of personal freedom in how social issues are expressed through business ventures. Some social entrepreneurs might be interested in certain social issues due to experience and this manifests in the social enterprise.

There are not many articles discussing social entrepreneurship in sport in a substantial manner, which has resulted in limited attempts to synthesize the integration of sport into social entrepreneurship research. Sport is a useful playground for social entrepreneurship due to its unique hybrid combination of public and private enterprise. Different theories regarding social entrepreneurship can be used in sport in order to explore its context.

Values associated with social entrepreneurship

Two key values associated with social entrepreneurship are compassion and moral obligation (Schwartz, 1994). This sense of societal duty is what differentiates social entrepreneurs from the rest of the population. As there is an ethic of care in the meaning of social entrepreneurship it is useful to see how it is conducted in a sport setting. The words "value" and "values" are crucial in our understanding of social entrepreneurship but they have very different meanings. Value is defined as "the creation or exchange of worth or utility in an economic sense" (Borquist and De Bruin, 2019:147). This emphasis on economics implies there is a financial association with value. In sport this is important as value connotes financial performance but can also have other meanings depending on the situation (Chen et al., 2019). For example, value can mean human capital in terms of an athlete's market worth or symbolic capital in terms of a team's brand reputation. In the plural sense, values are defined as "an ethical or normative meaning of prescribed or desired behavior, the 'moral compass' of an individual or society" (Borquist and De Bruin, 2019:147). Values are hard to define due to their abstract nature. This means they convey a sense of purpose in terms of what is important to a person (Deakins et al., 2007). This differs depending on individual attitudes towards way of behaving. Values incorporate a sense of moral obligation that an individual conforms to in their daily lives.

The main values associated with social entrepreneurship can be summarized as self-transcendence, openness to change and conservation (Borquist and De Bruin,

2019). Self-transcendence involves both benevolence and universalism due to the emphasis on helping others. Benevolence involves trying to look after others by being helpful and attentive. This is an important trait in social entrepreneurship as it places emphasis on being responsible. Other traits associated with benevolence involved forgiving others for mistakes and being loyal (Barak et al., 2016). These traits help an individual focus on the meaning of life through activities that bring them a sense of personal fulfillment. This includes taking a spiritual approach to what happens in a person's life and learning from experience. This helps preserve the social welfare of others and enhances the overall well-being of society.

Universalism involves having a sense of appreciation for the plight of others. Being tolerant and thoughtful about the needs of others helps build a more caring society. This is useful in ensuring that social justice and equality are issues that are addressed in society. It can also involve taking a holistic approach to world events that includes protecting democracy. Openness to change is a mindset that enables individuals to think through their actions in different ways. Being creative and independent with life choices can build a more cohesive society. This enables individuals to explore new paths by choosing avenues that are right for them. Conservation involves respecting the rights and beliefs of others. This involves a sense of harmony in ensuring the stability of society. Placing an emphasis on society in terms of a sense of belonging helps to shape future behaviors regarding social entrepreneurship.

Pattern processing is defined as "a cognitive process in which meaningful patterns are detected amongst seemingly unrelated events or trends" (Gray et al., 2019:328). Entrepreneurs utilize their imagination to understand patterns in the environment. Connecting seemingly unrelated events or occurrences can help establish a pattern. This in turn helps entrepreneurs identify opportunities in the market that are not currently captured. The process of discovering patterns occurs through some trial and error. This means there is a degree of experimentation in terms of what is being seen and understood. Vaghely and Julien (2010) found that cognitive patterns in the form of algorithms were useful in processing information. The way entrepreneurs use patterns depends on their ability to evaluate ideas based on environmental scanning.

Opportunities are identified in the market by searching for new ideas. This can occur in a planned or unplanned way depending on the preferences of the entrepreneur. Using planned searches by entrepreneurs is the approach taken by Schumpeter (1994). This means opportunities occur through a cognitive way in which information is evaluated by an entrepreneur. The process of discovery means that it is a deliberate way to gain knowledge about market potential. The Schumpeterian approach contrasts with the Kirznerian view, which suggests that no formal search is needed. Kirzner (1973) suggested that opportunities are discovered through entrepreneurs being alert to new needs. This means opportunities are created or enacted in the market by the entrepreneur. Another way to understand the process of entrepreneurship is by focusing on the knowledge asymmetries in the market. Hayek (1945) viewed how the key role of entrepreneurs is to make use of scarce resources by evaluating knowledge. This involves a bricolage approach as the resources that are available are used by entrepreneurs.

Social enterprises go beyond the traditional notions of organizations by pursuing public social goals with market-orientated techniques (Bhatt et al., 2019). Governments and non-profit organizations have typically been the ones interested in social problems in society. With increased privatization of services and deregulation there has been less money spent by governments on social issues. This has created a need in the market that has been partly filled by social enterprises. Social enterprises help socioeconomically disadvantaged sectors of society by providing help but through business ventures. This is different to non-profits who do not have a business model approach. Social enterprises have been a powerful tool in decreasing social inequality through productive change.

Jarrodi et al. (2019:1) define social entrepreneurs as "people who start up ventures either individually or as part of a startup team with the primary aim of achieving a social impact." The emphasis on social impact can be achieved in a number of different ways including through engagement with political systems. There are politics associated with social entrepreneurship due to the need to navigate institutional systems. This means that social entrepreneurs, whilst doing good, also have other motivations for acting in a pro-social way. This includes being an activist for a particular social cause that is influenced by an individual's ideology. Subversion theory has been used as a way to understand the political perspective of entrepreneurship. This is due to entrepreneurship being a way to socially transform communities. Bureau and Zander (2014) suggest that entrepreneurship is an act of subversion as the activity is motivated. However, this will depend on whether sport entities identify themselves as being social entrepreneurs.

Social identity theory

Social identity theory suggests that individuals associate themselves with certain traits or behaviors. This enables them to classify themselves into categories and shapes how they interact with others. This classification enables individuals to be members of certain groups as they share similar identities. The meanings that people place on their membership of a group are important. These meanings are formed by perceptions about positive and negative traits in a person. In social identity theory individuals desire to belong to a group that they share similar identities with. The identity is distinctive and helps distinguish members of one group from another. Normally individuals will want like-minded people in the same group and exclude those they consider to be different. Groups with a high social status will perceive themselves as having better personality traits than other groups. This leads to more self-esteem and the likelihood of others with similar traits wanting to join their group. Individuals have a psychological attachment to being a member of a group and this is important in sport teams, which develop based on group behavior. Members of sport teams categorize themselves based on group membership. Sport leaders help maintain the allure of group membership by drawing on their social identity. Effective sport leaders are able to harness the power of intergroup relations by focusing on relational social identity in terms of comparing how their sport team is identified in a certain way. Part of this comparison focuses on identity having a personal meaning.

Individuals belong to sport teams for a variety of reasons including geographic location, family tradition and for social enjoyment. Individuals have become members of sport teams due to their residing in the same geographic location or having an affinity for a physical place. This was traditionally how individuals became members of sport teams, as it was easier to watch and play sport in close geographic locations. This changed with people moving and living in different locations but the association is still there. Moreover, for some sport teams the geographic location also implies a social status, such as working class. Family tradition often means that membership of a sport team is given at birth. This has resulted in strong allegiance to sport teams and affected other parts of an individual's life, from their leisure activities to clothing. This has benefitted sport teams in their merchandising and sponsorship arrangements.

Sport has changed tremendously over the past decade due largely to entrepreneurial business endeavors. These changes have affected policy initiatives, but the pace of change is behind that occurring in practice. For this reason, it is important to take a new approach to sport policy by embedding an entrepreneurial perspective. This will help to make sport policy more dynamic in order to reflect the changes occurring in society. A social dilemma occurs when there is a conflict between personal versus collective benefits (Li et al., 2015). Due to the individualistic culture existing in many regions, social dilemmas may be perceived as normal occurrences. This means selfish decisions are considered part of an entrepreneur's behavior and needed in the competitive business environment. For some entrepreneurs, decisions that harm the collective good are not bad, but a by-product of an entrepreneur's actions. This perception has changed with the emphasis on social responsibility. There are a number of theories that focus on the way individuals interact in their social environment including social identity, social comparison and optimal distinctiveness.

The concept of community is at the heart of social entrepreneurship due to the central role that stakeholders play in strategic decision-making (Hill et al., 2010). In distressed communities social entrepreneurship is a necessity in order to help people in need. Sports organizations play a role in community economic development, particularly when they are connected to social enterprises. In order to build local community capacity sport enterprises can be an effective mechanism. Sport social enterprises can lead in value creation by facilitating self-help and employment opportunities in communities. The advantage of social entrepreneurs compared to purely non-profit initiatives is that they provide an income-generating service to support community development.

Dynamic capabilities are defined as "the ability of an organization and its management to build, to integrate and to reconfigure internal and external competencies to address complex and rapidly changing environments" (Al-Aali and Teece, 2014:104). In complex environments, the dynamic capabilities perspective has been used to identify appropriate opportunities. Having a timely response when opportunities are presented is important for sports organizations. Sports organizations need to employ their dynamic capabilities in order to remain competitive. This involves assessing viable opportunities to see potential lucrative business ventures.

Organizational fitness and sport

Organizational fitness can be described as the ability of an organization to adapt and survive in changing environments (Osborn and Hunt, 2007). Some organizations are more fit than others as they thrive on change. Others are less fit as they survive based on necessity and are reluctant to change. Lewin and Volberda (1999:520) define organizational fitness as the "correspondence between the adaptive behavioral capabilities of a class of organizations and their particular environment." The environment for an organization's fitness can be considered as simple or rugged (Meyer and Gauthier, 2013). Simple environments are easy to assess, as there tend to be predictable patterns. This results in activities tending to be easier to conduct due to the environment staying the same. In rugged environments there are changes that are harder to predict, which makes it difficult for organizations to navigate. These environments are characterized by changes that can be made more difficult when occurring through rapid technology changes. Organizations in rugged environments need to have some resilience in dealing with this changing behavior.

Sports organizations can vary in terms of their fitness based on a continuum from less fit to very fit. Having dynamic capabilities is a way that an organization can maintain its fitness as it enables it to be flexible with market demands. By actively engaging in their market environment, sports organizations can possess dynamic capabilities that are relevant to the changing environment. This enables them to contend with change in a way that is beneficial to their organization. Sports organizations that prosper tend to have a high level of fitness as they constantly learn and adapt.

Meyer and Gauthier (2013:23) state "social entrepreneurship offers a means by which the principles of businesses and organizations can be applied to improving the quality of life in our world." Quality of life is an increasing concern for citizens as they have become more interested in a work/life balance. There is more flexibility in the hours and locations where people work and this has resulted in changing economic geographies. At the same time organizations have encouraged more volunteering and philanthropic endeavors in work activity. This has led to social entrepreneurship becoming a promising way for citizens and organizations to unite on pressing social issues. Social entrepreneurship, unlike philanthropic or volunteering, involves some kind of financial return from the social business. This creates a feedback mechanism between the social entrepreneurs and community, which can further drive the growth of the social venture. For this reason, it is useful to think of social entrepreneurship as providing a benefit both to the people involved in starting and maintaining the social business but also the recipients who can feed back information.

In recent years, the sport sector has become an area of popularity for social entrepreneurship particularly as sports organizations move beyond just providing services to becoming more actively involved in the community. A way to understand how social entrepreneurship contributes to the quality of life is through focusing on how organizations adapt to social conditions. This is referred to as organizational fitness and is a useful term to understand the mechanisms of social entrepreneurship. To manage the fitness of a sports organization, there needs to be an assessment of how it is functioning and how it compares to other organizations. Whilst sports organizations are unique, there are still fitness goals that any form of organization needs to achieve. This competitiveness has intensified with the internationalization of sport, meaning information can be disseminated on a global scale. Organizations pursuing social entrepreneurship need to understand the ramifications of their activities in order to build more successful social ventures.

Vulnerability and social entrepreneurship

Social entrepreneurs seek to help marginalized sectors of society that are vulnerable. The concept of vulnerability refers to some degree of risk and usually relates to social disadvantage. There are individuals who are vulnerable due to their susceptibility to be harmed. This might occur as a result of poverty, a lack of education or through some other form of hardship. People have different coping capacities, depending on their intelligence and their use of available resources. In times of crisis some individuals are better able to adapt to their situation than others. Ranci (2010:16) defined vulnerability as "a situation that is characterized by a state of weakness which exposes a person or family to suffering particularly negative or damaging consequences if a problematic situation arises." Social welfare agencies have typically tried to help vulnerable people.

There are four main types of vulnerability that are relevant for social entrepreneurship: social, institutional, economic and environmental (Unceta et al., 2019). Social vulnerability is based on the assessment of risks due to societal conditions. This can influence an individual's exposure to other harmful events. Key indicators of social vulnerability include education, employment and health conditions. Socially vulnerable individuals face difficulties in obtaining access to services, which makes them likely to face adverse hardship. Institutional vulnerability involves an inability to voice concerns about structural conditions. This impacts on response rates and the way information is communicated. Some institutions are rigid and reluctant to change whilst others adapt at a rapid rate. The ability to respond to risky situations is an important feature needed in institutions, particularly in the dynamic marketplace. Institutions need to be accountable for the actions they take and this includes listening to the needs of citizens. Freedom of expression in a variety of forms, such as speech and media, is a way citizens can voice their opinions about institutions.

To be an effective institution there needs to be a degree of political independence. This enables policies to be formulated properly so that they utilize public services in an efficient manner. The credibility of policies will depend on the level of independence from political issues. There are rules of society that institutions need to follow. This derives from the government's ability to implement policies that contribute to the well-being of society. Promoting innovative policies can decrease the level of public power used for private gain. This is a way to regulate government interaction and help build confidence in the economy. Economic vulnerability infers a sensitivity to fluctuations in the marketplace. This occurs when there are risky situations in the market caused by financial instability. In order to lower the level of economic vulnerability there needs to be some degree of regulation in economic activity. This will strengthen the economic system and make it more resilient.

Environmental vulnerability involves potential dangerous use of natural resources. When environmental resources are being damaged then there needs to be management intervention to stop this happening. This can occur by different stakeholders trying to stop the degradation of natural resources in order to preserve resources for future generations. Sustainability is part of this objective as it enables appropriate environmental policies to be introduced and is an issue of interest for sports organizations particularly in terms of their interaction with the environment. There are three main dimensions of sustainability: "social equity (defined as equal access to resources), environmental integrity and economic prosperity" (Meyer and Gauthier, 2013:24). Social equity in a sport setting can mean a variety of things including fair pay and gender equity. However, most definitions of social equity in the lens of sustainability refer to economic or financial resources. Environmental integrity means being considerate of the space in which sport is played. Due to some sports requiring a high level of maintenance such as the watering and use of grass on playing fields, it is important to think about the resources used. There has been an increased focus on the use of water and other energy sources at sport games. In times of drought when the use of water is limited this has further restricted sport games. Economic prosperity focuses on the financial health of sports clubs and this has been a concern particularly for football clubs and teams. Football associations have introduced regulations about a club's financial performance in order to protect the reputation of the game.

Micro social enterprises refer to "very small, 'owner managed' enterprises." In emerging economies, micro social enterprises provide a way to address concerns in communities through mostly informal business activity. Micro social enterprises are able to cater for local community needs by being nimble. Bouchard (2012:50) defines a social innovation as

> an intervention initiated by social actors to respond to an aspiration, to meet specific needs, to offer a solution or to take advantage of an opportunity for action in order to modify social relations, transform a framework for action, or propose new cultural orientations.

Social innovations provide a way of seeing a problem in a new light.

Social enterprises make a significant contribution to the global economy. The social economy is defined as organizations, individuals and other entities that engage in economic activity that has a social component. The main objective of organizations in the social economy is to combine non-profit objectives with profit-making needs. The social economy includes

> building societies, charity trading arms, consumer retail societies, community businesses, credit unions, fair trade companies, housing associations, intermediate labour market companies, local exchange trading schemes, marketing cooperatives, mutual cooperative companies, social businesses, social firms, time banks, voluntary enterprises, workers cooperatives.
>
> *Smith, 2005:276*

This wide range of entities in the social economy shows the important economic element they play in society.

Fundraising in sport

Sports clubs, particularly local and amateur ones, have traditionally relied on fundraising as a source of revenue. The methods for fundraising have changed due to the increased usage of technology but the motives remain the same. As sports clubs have become larger, newer and more complex fundraising methods have emerged as a way to keep up with societal change. The aim of this chapter is to discuss the role that fundraising plays in social entrepreneurship. In sports clubs the model for fundraising is shifting to a social entrepreneurship one that focuses on profit creation (Gallagher et al., 2012). This change is a result of more emphasis on sustainable sources of financing. The aim of most fundraising initiatives in sport is to provide additional income for specific goals. This includes the building of new stadiums or supporting a social cause. Social entrepreneurship in sport has no universally accepted definition but most include a focus on social and financial objectives. This means the practice of social entrepreneurship can be considered as (1) entrepreneurship of sport activities or (2) entrepreneurship through sport. The first perspective suggests that entrepreneurship highlights the way to use existing sport structures, for example, innovative marketing or licensing partnerships, sponsorship agreements and fan associations. The second perspective focuses on the need to use sport to facilitate entrepreneurial activities, for example, using customer relationship management techniques from sports fans to buy related products and merchandise. Both perspectives rely on sport being the focal point of social entrepreneurship. Sports organizations have always tended to have a social orientation, which makes them useful structures for social entrepreneurship. This social emphasis is evident in a sports organization being defined as "a social entity involved in the sports industry; it is goal directed, with a consciously structured activity system and a relatively identifiable boundary" (Slack and Parent, 2006:5). The degree to which a sports organization is involved with social entrepreneurship is determined by its entrepreneurial orientation but also its attitude towards social change. Sports organizations can range in size from small non-profits, larger for-profits and publicly owned entities.

Fundraising has been used by sports organizations to supplement their existing budgets and provide new sources of income. In a sport context, fundraising normally refers to conducting an activity that results in monetary gain. It is generally considered as a concept that refers to obtaining resources for a social goal. The emphasis on social initiatives is implicit in most definitions, although this might not always be the case. Rosso (1991:4) takes a positive approach to defining fundraising by stating it is "the gentle art of teaching people the joy of giving." This description implies that people enjoy giving to others because they receive a warm feeling (Gallagher et al., 2012). There are also other reasons for giving that have an altruistic rationale, including helping others and giving back to society. The circular economy in which goods are recycled and reused can be linked to the concept of fundraising. This is due to more emphasis being placed on sustainability and environmental initiatives. Other less altruistic reasons are networking, prestige and recognition. In a sports setting, this is important as individuals can alleviate their status in society by being seen as philanthropic. There is also the positive media associated with fundraising that can benefit people who like to network. Fundraising brings together a group of people for a common cause and in the process relies on shared bonding. This means people become acquainted with others in the pursuit of a common goal. The benefits of this networking can lead to new opportunities but can also build a person's self-esteem.

Communication is the main way information about a fundraising event is spread through the community. Fundraising involves sharing knowledge about a charitable cause and how donations can contribute to solving social problems (Kelly 1998:107). Thus, social issues that need to be solved can be brought to people's attention by going to fundraising events. Increasingly, sport has been used as a fundraising platform due to the physical as well as societal benefits that can result. This includes fun runs that aim to raise money but also involves physical activity. Fundraising in sport has become more creative in terms of these events because of the location, structure and prizes.

Fundraising, whilst normally considered a one-off event, can also be linked to other areas of interest. This includes sport maintenance programs that rely on the development of a public/private partnership. Therefore, the fundraising can refer to a holistic strategy. Lindahl (2010:4) takes this approach by stating that fundraising is "the creation and ongoing development of relationships between a not-for-profit organization and its various donors for the purpose of increasing gift revenue to the organization." Thus, the focus is on the sports organization as the main conduit for the flow of information related to the fundraising activity.

Conclusion

There is a need to reform sport policy to take into account emerging challenges. Whilst sport policy has always been progressive there are some elements that are lagging and need to be readdressed. Sport is now a billon dollar global industry that combines amateur and professional sporting bodies. This combination of profit and non-profit sports associations means that entrepreneurship can be used as a way to facilitate creative thinking. Creativity is valued in business and the sports industry needs to use creativity in order to embrace change. In addition, the changing circumstances for many sport authorities means they need to be more self-sufficient and rely less on government funding. Sport entrepreneurship is still a new concept in the policy world despite its usefulness and practicality. The entrepreneurship field provides a useful base from which to develop better sport policy. This will help shape new sport policy by suggesting creative solutions to policy difficulties.

Get policy on national agenda to get more funding for community work.

References

Al-Aali, A. and Teece, D. (2014) "International entrepreneurship and the theory of the (long-lived) international firm: A capabilities perspective," *Entrepreneurship Theory & Practice*, January: 95–116.

Anderson, A., Younis, S., Hashim, H. and Air, C. (2019) "Social enterprising informing our concept: Exploring informal micro social enterprise," *Social Enterprise Journal*, 15(1): 94–100.

Barak, M., Lizano, E., Kim, A., Duan, L., Rhee, M., Hsiao, H. and Brimhall, L. (2016) "The promise of diversity management for climate of inclusion: A state of the art review and meta-analysis," *Human Service Organizations: Management, Leadership & Governance*, 40(4): 305–333.

Bhatt, B., Qureshi, I. and Riaz, S. (2019) "Social entrepreneurship in non-munificent institutional environments and implications for institutional work: Insight from China," *Journal of Business Ethics*, 154: 605–630.

Borquist, B. and De Bruin, A. (2019) "Values and women-led social entrepreneurship," *International Journal of Gender and Entrepreneurship*, 11(2): 146–165.

Bouchard, M. (2012) "Social innovation, an analytical grid for understanding the social economy: The example of the Quebec housing sector," *Service Business*, 6: 47–59.

Bureau, S. and Zander, I. (2014) "Entrepreneurship as an act of subversion," *Scandinavian Journal of Management*, 30(1): 124–133.

Chen, W., Tajeddini, K., Ratten, V. and Tabari, S. (2019) "Educational immigrants: Evidence from Chinese young entrepreneurs in the UK," *Journal of Enterprising Communities: People and Places in the Global Economy*, 13(1/2): 196–215.

Deakins, D., Ishaq, M., Smallbone, D., Whittam, G. and Wyper, J. (2007) "Ethnic minority businesses in Scotland and the role of social capital," *International Small Business Journal*, 25(3): 307–326.

Ferreira, J. J. M., Fernandes, C. I. and Ratten, V. (2016) "A co-citation bibliometric analysis of strategic management research," *Scientometrics*, 109(1): 1–32.

Gallagher, D., Gilmore, A. and Stolz, A. (2012) "The strategic marketing of small sport clubs: From fundraising to social entrepreneurship," *Journal of Strategic Marketing*, 20(3): 231–247.

Gray, B., Kirkwood, J., Monahan, E. and Etemaddar, M. (2019) "Internal factors influencing effective opportunity identification in a Tongan social enterprise," *Journal of Small Business & Entrepreneurship*, 31(4): 323–347.

Hayek, F. (1945) "The use of knowledge in society," *The American Economic Review*, 35(4): 519–530.

Hill, T., Kothari, T. and Shea, M. (2010) "'Patterns' of meaning in the social entrepreneurship literature: A research platform," *Journal of Social Entrepreneurship*, 1(1): 5–31.

Jarrodi, H., Byrne, J. and Bureau, S. (2019) "A political ideology lens on social entrepreneurship motivations," *Entrepreneurship & Regional Development*, in press, 1–22.

Kelly, K. S. (1998) *Effective fund-raising management*. Mahwah, NJ: Lawrence Erlbaum.

Kirzner, I. (1973) *Competition and entrepreneurship*. Chicago, IL: University of Chicago Press.

Lewin, A. Y. and Volberda, H. W. (1999) "Prolegomena on coevolution: A framework for research on strategy and new organizational forms," *Organization Science*, 10(5): 519–534.

Li, Y., Yao, F. and Ahlstrom, D. (2015) "The social dilemma of bribery in emerging economies: A dynamic model of emotion, social value and institutional uncertainty," *Asia Pacific Journal of Management*, 32: 311–334.

Lindahl, W. (2010) *Principles of fundraising: Theory and practice*. Burlington, MA: Jones & Bartlett Learning.

Meyer, C. and Gauthier, J. (2013) "Navigating challenging fitness landscapes: Social entrepreneurship and the competing dimensions of sustainability," *Journal of Social Entrepreneurship*, 4(1): 23–39.

Osborn, R. N. and Hunt, J. G. J. (2007) "Leadership and the choice of order: Complexity and hierarchical perspectives near the edge of chaos," *The Leadership Quarterly*, 18(4): 319–340.

Ranci, C. (ed.) (2010) "Social vulnerability in Europe," in *Social Vulnerability in Europe* (pp. 3–24). London: Palgrave Macmillan.

Ratten, V. (2019) "Social innovation in sport: The creation of Santa Cruz as a world surfing reserve," *International Journal of Innovation Science*, 11(1): 20–30.

Ratten, V. and Jones, P. (2018) "Future research directions for sport education: Toward an entrepreneurial learning approach," *Education + Training*, 60(5): 490–499.

Ratten, V., Ferreira, J. and Fernandes, C. (2016) "Entrepreneurial and network knowledge in emerging economies: A study of the global entrepreneurship monitor," *Review of International business and Strategy*, 26(3): 392–409.

Rosso, H. (1991) *Achieving excellence in fund raising*. San Francisco, CA: Jossey-Bass.

Schumpeter, J. (1994) *Capitalism, Socialism and Democracy*. London: Routledge.

Schwartz, S. (1994) "Are there universal aspects in the structure and contents of human values?" *Journal of Social Issues*, 50(4): 19–45.

Slack, T. and Parent, M. M. (2006) *Understanding sport organizations: The application of organization theory*. Champaign, IL: Human Kinetics.

Smith, G. (2005) "Green citizenship and the social economy," *Environmental Politics*, 14(2): 273–289.

Unceta, A., Luna, A., Castro, J. and Wintjes, R. (2019) "Social innovation regime: An integrated approach to measure social innovation," *European Planning Studies*, in press, 1–19.

Vaghely, I. and Julien, P. (2010) "Are opportunities recognized or constructed? An information perspective on entrepreneurial opportunity identification," *Journal of Business Venturing*, 25(1): 73–86.

3

PROCESSES AND MECHANISMS FOR SOCIAL ENTREPRENEURSHIP

Introduction

In contrast to the growing research on social entrepreneurship in general, sport social entrepreneurship has received little attention. This contrasts with increased emphasis on social entrepreneurship in specific contexts such as emerging markets. Greater attention is needed in the research area of sport and social entrepreneurship due to its practical significance but also in the way it can influence other fields of study. When social entrepreneurship is studied in a sport context both the sport and social parts are core elements. The "social" element of sport social entrepreneurship means that the business activity has a social process in character and structure. This refers to social objectives in terms of overall performance outcomes, which are at the heart of the definition. Social outcomes can include societal progression, empowerment and inclusion. The key emphasis is on cohesion and the way social capital can be built through its link to sport. When the word "sport" is added it has an emphasis on improving the quality of sport services and products through social means (Costa, 2005). This normally involves focusing on the quality of life for participants and overall social welfare.

Social entrepreneurship has become of strategic importance for sports organizations wanting to capitalize on their reputation by building social connections in the market. Despite the impact social entrepreneurship can have on the performance of sports organizations, the literature on social entrepreneurship takes a general view without considering the intricacies of the sports industry. Social entrepreneurship needs to be integrated with a sport firm's strategy in order to facilitate alignment with their strategic plans. From a managerial point of view, sports organizations perform better when they can show a social alignment with community values. More sports organizations are adopting a community perspective when undertaking social projects. As sports clubs can be both amateur and professional, it helps them to identify with community goals when engaging in social endeavors. Social enterprises can take a variety of forms, from for-profit enterprises that have a social mission to non-government organizations. This means that social entrepreneurs can be judged based on the transformation goal and community need they service. Some sports-related social entrepreneurs have a social objective as part of their program but often social entrepreneurs use whatever resources they have available to solve issues.

Social entrepreneurship has a wider market appeal in sport besides its community advantages as it promotes thinking in a social manner (Potts and Ratten, 2016). This appeal means it is useful to analyze the processes and mechanisms for social entrepreneurship as a way to build research in a sport context. The social entrepreneurship process should be incorporated into the whole sport value chain from the sourcing of materials to the production of goods (Ratten, 2011). This is important, as sports organizations have diversified into different market segments in order to grow their profitability. Part of this success has been attributed to the social networks existing in the sports industry that enable leveraging of brand value and reputation (Atuahene-Gima and Wei, 2011). The social network approach in entrepreneurship suggests "entrepreneurs are embedded into social contexts that influence the decisions which they take, and this influences the chances of successfully completing their plans" (Klyver and Foley, 2012:561). These social networks are crucial in sport, which largely relies on the personal connections and emotional attachments people have with sport.

Despite the plethora of social networks existing in the sports industry, sports organizations need to be motivated to engage in social entrepreneurship. This is due to there being evidence that socially engaged sports organizations are more important in economies than those without a social conscious. Traditional sports organizations are only associated with the practice of sport whereas social sport enterprises, in contrast, are involved in pressing social issues. Thus, sport social enterprises can be analyzed in terms of usage, knowledge, stakeholders and policy considerations (Kim and Lui, 2015). The usages include facilitating broader social engagement in terms of alleviating problems in society (Dyllick and Hockerts, 2002). This means the reasons for the social enterprise in a sport setting need to be defined in a clear way. Thereby, the description and reason for needing a specific sport social enterprise are required to understand market feasibility. This will enable the social enterprise to reach set goals but also increase, if needed, their engagement in the community. Knowledge characteristics involve the level of intellectual property and research required for the social enterprise to function properly (Davenport and Prusak, 1998). More social enterprises are using online platforms to facilitate better social interaction. This helps both online and physical environments to derive better functionality through sport experiences. Stakeholder considerations refer to the different types of participants needed whilst policy considerations refer more to government agendas involving sport.

The main streams of social entrepreneurship in sport research can be divided into (1) classification and definition, (2) process and mechanisms, (3) evaluation and outcome and (4) implications and performance. The first stream focuses on understanding how social entrepreneurship is different in a sport context and what it is that makes it distinctive. This involves conceptualizing social entrepreneurship in a way that makes it integral to the functioning of the sports industry. To do this unpacking the core elements of social entrepreneurship in sport are needed as there is a time lag between the way social entrepreneurship is practiced and researched in academia. Thus, it will take some time to understand how social entrepreneurship can be delivered in sport settings. The second stream involves the process of social entrepreneurship and the mechanisms required to make it happen (Fedele and Miniac, 2010).

Often social entrepreneurs have distinctive leadership qualities that make what they do and say important. In sport there is a fundamental underpinning on competitiveness that drives the way people behave inside and outside of an organizational setting. Thus, it is necessary to focus on the leadership capabilities of social entrepreneurs to understand how these attributes can be managed in the sports industry. This involves learning about the mechanisms and steps needed to make social entrepreneurship a reality. In the past, sports organizations were involved in many voluntary or pro-bono activities but this has changed with the realization that non-profit activities can also have a business element (Jones et al., 2017). This is where social entrepreneurship fills the gap in the market between non-profit and profit activities that enable a new form of business model innovation to emerge (Foss and Saebi, 2017).

The third stream is about the evaluation and outcomes of social entrepreneurship. This means identifying what is and what is not working in terms of social entrepreneurship and how it applies to sport. To do this, it can be helpful to describe how social entrepreneurship occurs and the steps that are required to obtain a certain outcome (Hansmann, 1980). The evaluation process can be difficult as the benefits of social entrepreneurship can take time to come to fruition. This requires that the different stages or components of social entrepreneurship need to be understood as a work in progress (Kirby, 2004). The outcomes of social entrepreneurship are also subjective and dependent sometimes on the timing and needs of individuals. Thus, for some, social entrepreneurship in sport might be a continual learning process that leads to the development of good partnerships whilst for others it can involve specific development goals. For this reason it is helpful to have a social development plan in process in order to monitor each step. The fourth stream is about the implications and performance of social entrepreneurship in sport. The implications depend on the setting and behaviors of the people involved in social entrepreneurship (Brockner et al., 2004). There is a difference between the types of implications as social, financial and community considerations need to be taken into account. Implications can be delineated in terms of relevance and their contribution to the overall experience of social entrepreneurship in sport. Furthermore, the way social entrepreneurship is interpreted in terms of conceptual and theoretical application needs to be taken into account. This involves assessing the main focus of social entrepreneurship before reaching a conclusion (Gërguri-Rashiti et al., 2017). Some of the implications will partly overlap in terms of community and social relevance so they need to be scrutinized for accuracy.

This chapter is structured as follows. First, the processes that facilitate social entrepreneurship in sport are stated. Next, the mechanisms needed for social entrepreneurship to function properly are discussed in terms of functionality and performance. The example of the fitness industry and its changing entrepreneurial nature is then examined, which gives a good example of both the processes and mechanisms of sport-based social entrepreneurship.

Processes for social entrepreneurship

Sports organizations have a number of networks that can facilitate the process of social entrepreneurship. The most relevant external networks are market and institutional ones that are needed to facilitate the flow of information dissemination. Knowledge is needed for learning and network partners in terms of how they contribute to bring diverse ideas and resources into the marketplace (Jones et al., 2018). In order to assess knowledge it is useful to involve a blue ocean strategy, which is a phrase coined for its focus on finding uncontested market spaces (Agnihotri, 2015). Within the blue ocean strategy, the ERRC approach (elimination, reduction, raise and creation) has been utilized to find potentially untapped market needs (Kim and Mauborgne, 2005). This approach can be used in a sport setting to find ways to eliminate social inequality by reducing poverty. In addition, social entrepreneurship can raise the profile of non-profit endeavors by creating new opportunities.

Sports organizations are setting a new precedent for social entrepreneurship by developing new ideas. Especially in resource-constrained environments, social entrepreneurship provides a way to maximize costs by innovating in an efficient manner for a social purpose. This has enticed practitioners to use more social entrepreneurship in sport as sports organizations are pervasive in economic growth and influence a number of other sectors. Compared to other types of organizations, sports organizations are believed to have a more entrepreneurial learning approach due to their need to constantly improve. As a distinctive type of business sports organizations emphasize innovation and how they can utilize knowledge to adapt to changing market conditions.

The significance of sport enterprises as well as ancillary businesses to the economic conditions of a region is undeniable. Managing resources together with good strategic planning skills is essential for sports organizations. Firm resources include a range of both tangible and intangible assets including capabilities, capital, knowledge and processes (Alonso and Bressan, 2016). Social entrepreneurship is different to general forms of entrepreneurship due to the emphasis on social issues and use of resources. The transformation of sports organizations to social enterprises is an outcome of the shift in society towards social goals. As a consequence, more sports organizations are embedding social entrepreneurship within their management systems as a core activity in order to deal with changing markets.

Concerned markets are conceptualized as a manifestation of society in terms of what is needed and actions required (Geiger et al., 2014). This acknowledges the multiple and often competing interests of stakeholders in society. In contemporary markets there are different needs and wants of citizens, which contribute to community development. D'Antone et al. (2017) suggest that there are processes to both let and integrate concern into markets. The steps needed to let concerns enter the market include relating, troubling and influencing (D'Antone et al., 2017). This means that sports organizations need to relate to the social issues in their community that are troubling their stakeholders. As sports entities normally hold prestigious or powerful positions in society they can influence others by engaging in social entrepreneurship. This can involve a number of different steps including architectural management (Lusch and Vargo, 2014). This means focusing on the way a sports organization is governed and the value it brings to society. The different products/services/processes that a sports organization is involved with in terms of at the community or international level needs to be analyzed. This will lead to a better understanding of how sport social enterprises make money and their value orientation. Table 3.1 below states in more detail the ways social entrepreneurship can be understood in sports organizations and the questions they need to ask.

To understand how social entrepreneurship is embedded in sports organizations it is useful to focus on their business models. There are a variety of ways to conceptualize business models as they are part of the strategic management literature and are prone to continual improvement (Philipson, 2016). A seminal definition is provided by Teece (2010:172) who defined business models as "the manner by which the enterprise delivers value to customers, entices customers to pay for value and converts those payments to profit." This definition has been used because it references customers and value as being the focal area of inquiry and is useful

TABLE 3.1 Social entrepreneurship model

Social entrepreneurship component	Questions to ask
Architectural management	How is the sport social enterprise configured and managed?
	What is the governance structure?
	What kind of value creation mechanisms exist for the sport social enterprise?
Products/services/processes	What does the sport social enterprise sell?
	Is the sport social enterprise focused on the community or the international level?
Revenue model	How does the sport social enterprise make money?
	What level of profitability is required for the sport social enterprise to function properly?
Value orientation	What is special or distinctive about the sport social enterprise?

TABLE 3.2 Adjustment strategies in response to social problems

1. Move to introduce entrepreneurial thinking
2. Incorporate more diverse thinking to solve problems
3. Reduce reliance on government funding and subsidies
4. Reorientate business to be a social business
5. Seek help from the community
6. Develop strategic partnerships with local stakeholders
7. Reorganize business to be more productive and efficient

in a sport context. Broadly speaking, business models involve the overall mission of an enterprise in terms of what it does and the goals it needs to achieve. Each business has a different architecture depending on the industry it is in. Thus, business models evolve but are used as a tool to help managers communicate and design change processes (Osterwalder and Pigneur, 2010). This includes analyzing market fluctuations as a way to capture the essential essence of their business (Martin and Sunley, 2015). Another way to understand business models is through the way problems are identified and solved. Baden-Fuller and Haefliger (2013:419) define a business model as "a system that solves the problem of identifying who is (or are) the customer(s), engaging with their needs, delivering satisfaction and monetarizing the value." This definition is useful in understanding the markets that sports organizations need to be involved in when strategically planning their future, and how it is necessary for them to adjust to changing societal needs (Vamplew, 2019). Table 3.2 below states how sports organizations can change in response to social problems by building social enterprises.

Social entrepreneurship in sport is distinctive and should not be generalized to other industry settings. The sports industry has been a recipient of social entrepreneurship due to its ability to interact with members of the community. Generating a better understanding of how social entrepreneurship in sport works is important for building the sports industry (Miloch et al., 2012). However, there are different biases and perceptions of social entrepreneurship due to its comparison with other types of entrepreneurship. The actual and future behavior of sports organizations towards social entrepreneurship needs to be considered. It may be difficult to gather information about intentions towards social entrepreneurship, so different time periods including the present and future need to be considered (Ratten, 2009). This would enable a study of the interaction effects between intending to engage, and actually engaging, in social entrepreneurship. In sport, social entrepreneurship is perceived as a practice created area as it can bring a non-profit and volunteering perspective.

Social entrepreneurship is a way sports organizations can bring about positive social change, which is defined as

> the process of transforming patterns of thought, behavior, social relationships, institutions, and social structure to generate beneficial outcomes for

> individuals, communities, organizations, society and/or the environment beyond the benefits for the instigators of such transformations.
>
> *Stephan et al., 2016:1252*

This definition implies that there are a variety of ways sports organizations bring about positive social change depending on the perceptions of individuals involved in the change. As the sports industry impacts the economy in a number of different ways, including through worldwide retail sales and purchases of related services, it is important to take this into consideration when designing social entrepreneurship programs. Kim and James (2016:228) state "the retail sales of licensed merchandise of Major League Baseball were $5.5 billion in 2013. Sales by the Collegiate Licensing Company were $4.59 billion in 2013 and sales for the National Football League in 2013 were 3.25 billion." This means that sport products that embed a spirit of social entrepreneurship are likely to have an impact on sales figures.

Mechanisms for social entrepreneurship

Social entrepreneurship is still an emergent topic in the world of sport. The developmental nature of the literature means that researchers need to shape the contours of the field by bringing in ideas from practice. This will help move the literature forward by suggesting research topics and expand the breadth of the literature. There are diverse approaches that the research on social entrepreneurship in sport can take, which means this chapter will be of use to sports managers and policymakers by encouraging them to focus more on social entrepreneurship (Ratten, 2012). There can be little doubt that entrepreneurship in sport is becoming one of the most important ways of understanding change. Social forms of entrepreneurship are emerging within the literature as a way to bridge the non-profit motivations of sport entities. Given the breadth of social entrepreneurship issues in sport there are a number of ways to contribute to the literature and assist researchers with familiarizing themselves on the work on social entrepreneurship in sport (Ratten, 2015).

Sport is often understood from a competitive perspective rather than a purely leisure activity. The way people view sport will depend on their position in the sport system. There are a number of steps involved in developing social entrepreneurship in sport. Step one involves having the motivation and this underpins the whole approach to entrepreneurship (Ratten, 2014). Many individuals will actively seek out social issues and embody this in their attitude towards sport-related activities. In order to sustain motivation there are times that an individual will need to reverse and have adequate recovery in order to advance in the future. Thus, being goal-orientated and self-disciplined can help an individual set out to become a social entrepreneur (Ratten, 2018a). Having the right training and preparation is important in ensuring that they focus on social issues. As some social issues may be emotional it is important to carefully consider the actions needed (Ratten and Ferreira, 2016). This involves developing the right emotional state that can support a competitive attitude.

The importance of social entrepreneurship in sport has repeatedly been stated by local, national and international policy authorities. Sport is an activity often viewed by policy planners as a way to incorporate social goals, especially when other parts of the economy are lagging (Ratten, 2018b). The key idea behind entrepreneurship involves getting things done using available resources. Entrepreneurship involves an activity continuum as it incorporates different intensities from low to high involvement. Incorporating social entrepreneurship within sports organizations is a complex process as it may require strategic changes. This is evident with Zeimers et al. (2019:81) who state that sports organizations need "to respond to wider social issues and demonstrate their respectability to deliver social good both within and outside the sporting sphere." This respectability is a key component of the sports industry that has a large number of non-profit or amateur organizations in addition to profit-orientated international organizations.

The concept of entrepreneurship has broadened from just an economic activity to incorporate family, lifestyle and social goals (Dawson et al., 2011). A lifestyle business involves "a scenario where the owner/proprietor either balances his/her economic and non-economic goals or is primarily motivated by a set of lifestyle aspirations that are given a higher priority than economic objectives" (Dawson et al., 2011:552). Social entrepreneurship is a lifestyle for many individuals involved in sport. Unlike other industries, there is a large amateur and non-profit component in sport, which involves a large number of unpaid and volunteer labor (Godbey et al., 2005). This means social issues and causes are important to these people because of their interest in lifestyle factors. Lifestyle entrepreneurs are defined as "individuals who owned and operated businesses closely aligned with their personal values, interests and passions" (Marcketti et al., 2006:241). Lifestyle entrepreneurship whilst commonly used in a tourism context has been less used in sport studies (Goulding et al., 2005). This is interesting as sport is a lifestyle for many individuals and represents a way of life. Compared to traditional entrepreneurs, lifestyle entrepreneurs focus on personal interests and circumstances. Often social entrepreneurship is a way for individuals involved in sport activities to pursue personal goals. As sport was traditionally a leisure activity, although this has recently changed, it makes sense to link social issues to sport endeavors (Hudson et al., 2019). The goal of lifestyle entrepreneurs is to "succeed at living a certain quality of life by maintaining an income which allows them to survive" (Marchant and Mottiar, 2011:172). This focus on quality of life is important in social entrepreneurship, which focuses on issues that have a lifestyle implication in terms of social need (Kalantaridis and Bika, 2006).

Douglas and Prentice (2019:69) state "the three 'main pillars' of the social entrepreneurship literature are prosocial motivation, innovation and profit making." Having a prosocial motivation means that individuals want to contribute to alleviating social problems through innovation. As part of this motivation there needs to be a financial objective in that the business venture will result in profits. Thus, sport funding bodies need to screen applicants for social entrepreneurship funding on the basis of creativity and innovation. The attitudes of the applications towards finding novel social solutions to problems is important and social entrepreneurs need to be trained to view sport as a good context because of its link with the community. Policymakers should teach how to be a social entrepreneur in sport, emphasizing the unique advantages of the sports industry.

To promote the positive health benefits associated with sport it needs to be accessible, adaptable and build capacity (Edwards and Rowe, 2019). What is meant by accessible is that all sectors of society, including rich and poor, should be able to play sport. This is referred to sometimes as sport for all as it empowers disadvantaged members of society to play sport thereby leveling the playing field. Community needs are paramount in ensuring sport is accessible and can involve subsidies or grants. Being adaptable means that sport changes to reflect new needs in society. In the past, sport was played in man-made settings designed specifically for the sport. For example, cricket pitches and football fields that were shaped in the size required for the game. More ad hoc and natural settings such as the beach for surfing or mountains for rock climbing are now being used. Building capacity means getting more people involved in sport through watching or participating in sport.

Social business learning approaches

Social entrepreneurship in sport is not a new concept as it has been practiced in sport for some time but under different names, such as social business partnerships. The value of social entrepreneurship is that it can be created by an organization to help others, which is useful in the sports industry. The social orientation of many sports organizations is a relevant starting point for social entrepreneurship. In addition, the social tendencies of sports organizations have a bearing on their use of social entrepreneurship, which can be traced back to the reasons why individuals become entrepreneurs. Frank Knight's theory of entrepreneurship focuses on entrepreneurs as those who exercise judgment based on uncertainty when making decisions (Knight, 1921). This has been referred to as "Knightian uncertainty" due to the emphasis on probability and future orientated actions (Yang and Andersson, 2018). In Knight's theory uncertainty is acknowledged but needs to be assessed based on future scenarios. This approach has been used in economic modeling as a way to estimate courses of action.

The sense of social purpose is embedded in social entrepreneurship because it involves societal change. Murphy and Coombes (2009:326) define social entrepreneurship as the "recognition of a convergence of social, economic, and environmental resources allowing potential introduction of new goods, services, raw materials, markets and/or means-ends relations as an organized venture intended to generate social, economic and/or environmental value amidst circumstances of mobilization." This lengthy definition acknowledges social entrepreneurship as being a complex phenomena with a variety of different inputs and outputs. This is supported by Yeh et al. (2016:1206) who assert that "social entrepreneurship is a term that can be used to describe a wide variety of activities that amalgamate for-profit and idealistic purposes." Due to the complex nature of social entrepreneurship it helps to understand it from a social business perspective.

The five main ways to understand social business are: missions and outcomes, characteristics, operational aspects, resource utilization and environmental considerations (Ashraf et al., 2019). (1) Mission and outcomes refer to the emphasis on social issues with regards to solving problems. Social business values shape society through the involvement of innovation and passion. (2) Characteristics refer to how an enterprise is viewed by others in society. Social businesses focus on creating value through interventionist approaches that aid societal development. (3) Operational aspects refer to the business strategies used that enable better financial performance. Having the right approach to social marketing and business management is important. (4) Resource utilization refers to the quality and type of inputs needed in a social business, which includes the sharing of resources through investments and partnerships. (5) Environmental considerations refer to the way social businesses consider the land and use of natural resources. In order to understand social entrepreneurship in sport from a social business perspective it is useful to highlight the learning approaches. This includes benchmarking the social enterprise compared to other sport enterprises, then focusing on customer development and experimentation. This is facilitated by processes specifically targeted at social entrepreneurship that can facilitate future training initiatives in sports organizations on how to integrate social entrepreneurship. This is summarized in Table 3.3 below.

The past experience and history of sports organizations has an impact on their perception of social entrepreneurship. To build more social enterprises in sport there should be a motivation of the people involved to utilize the heritage of sports organizations by focusing on social endeavors. This can occur by focusing on intrapreneurship as well as entrepreneurship. Neesson et al. (2018:7) define intrapreneurship as

> a process whereby employee(s) recognize and exploit opportunities by being innovative, proactive and by taking risks in order for the organisation to create new products, processes and services, initiate self-renewal or venture new businesses to enhance the competitiveness and performance of the organization.

Due to the number of people involved in sport, including athletes, managers, coaches, fans and spectators, it is useful to consider the internal workings of a sports organization to see what kind of entrepreneurship can occur. This differs from the traditional forms of entrepreneurship, which focus on outside endeavors, that a sports organization can be involved with.

Social entrepreneurship is distinct from traditional organizational practices as it focuses on the business behaviors that utilize a social responsibility perspective. For sports organizations to be proactive they need to consider social entrepreneurship as a renewal process. This means developing social proactive work-related initiatives

TABLE 3.3 Learning approaches to social entrepreneurship in sport

Learning approach	Sport examples
Benchmarking	Comparing the social enterprise to other organizations in sport.
	Determining how well the social enterprise performs compared to sports industry averages.
Competency development	Acquiring knowledge and skills for the sport social enterprise.
	Recruiting people to help build the sport social enterprise.
Continuous improvement	Having a constant flow of information about how to progress the social enterprise.
	Learning from mistakes by engaging in total quality management practices.
Customer development	Involving customers as part of the co-creation process to learn new ideas.
	Improving products through having mixed teams of both customers and developers.
Experimentation	Trying new business practices and ideas.
	Having a clear purpose about what the sport social enterprise should achieve and how performance can be improved.
Processes	Implementing dynamic changes to how a social enterprise operates in sport.
	Collaborating with other firms and individuals to further the progress of the sport social enterprise.
Training	Incorporating education programs aimed at developing new skills related to social entrepreneurship and sport.
	Introducing new ways of thinking about social problems in sport.

to pursue new opportunities. By departing from previous practices social entre-preneurship can enable organizations to be more responsive to social issues in the environment. To be a social entrepreneur requires a certain skill set that encourages new idea creation by being assertive about required changes. Some ideas need to be initiated and then refined in the marketplace. This involves acquiring the right knowledge but then also experimenting with what does or does not work. Having some tolerance of failure can help organizations take opportunities that take time to develop. There are a number of outcomes from social entrepreneurship including innovation, increased productivity and better performance. As there has been more emphasis on work/life balance, integrating social issues into business activities can provide sports organizations with a way to connect to their environment. Pressing social issues can be incorporated into the marketing efforts of sports organizations and implemented through appropriate strategies.

Strategic sport policy

There is a need to study alternative approaches to social entrepreneurship through a sport lens. The stereotypical perception of social entrepreneurship being the same in all industries needs to change. There needs to be an analysis of the meaning of social entrepreneurship and how it applies to sport firms. Social entrepreneurship has a political component as it requires sports organizations to focus on certain social issues. This means an understanding about how power and privilege affect the sports industry is needed. Social entrepreneurship as a policy can legitimize sports organizations' strategic direction towards social issues. But it can also obscure the real reason sports organizations are interested in a social issue. Thus, a close collaboration between sports organizations and social policy practitioners is needed to develop better social entrepreneurship practices. This includes assessing how social entrepreneurship practices can reduce inequality.

A better awareness about inequality in society and the role sports organizations play in this process is needed. Whilst sport has positive societal benefits, it can also create inequality amongst those who can and cannot play sport. This is where social entrepreneurship policy can lessen the inequality by explicitly addressing this gap. To do this, privileged members of sports organizations that have social prestige can become involved in social entrepreneurship practices. It is not an easy task so there needs to be buy-in from the upper management levels of sports organizations. This will encourage a top down approach to social entrepreneurship that can then lead to a more collaborative environment. For retired athletes, this can also be a way for them to leverage social connections but also advance social justice and equality. As athletes, whether still playing sport or retired, have a privileged status in society, their presence can help to promote social entrepreneurship causes. The concept of privileged work can be linked to the work athletes do. Dennissen et al. (2018:19) state "privilege work entails an ongoing reflection on one's privileged status as well as the relationship to the underprivileged." For many individuals connected to sport, they have a privileged position in society that means any social activities they engage in will be recognized as being important in the community.

All levels of employees, from front line to managers, can induce socially inspired enterprise in sports organizations. By leveraging the connection a sports organization has in its community, social enterprises can spark larger changes. Thus, sports organizations need to use new logics and tactics to start and develop social enterprises. Rather than reacting to social change, sports organizations need to be proactive about starting social enterprises. This can enable them to adapt to the changing business environment by adopting a social change role.

The literature devoted to social entrepreneurship is already voluminous due to the increased interest in this area of study. Despite the large number of articles, books and reports on social entrepreneurship, there is some uncertainty about its meaning in the sports industry. This derives from sports organizations already being involved in many social projects that tend to be more non-profit initiatives rather than ones with a profit orientation. This has created a lack of definitional precision about social entrepreneurship in sport and unresolved discussion about its precise meaning. Social entrepreneurship in sport is reflective in many ways of policy intervention. Government policy at the local, state, national and international levels has tended to focus more on social outcomes of sport and less on integrating business practices. Newer policy interventions have changed perspective by arguing for more business outcomes of sport social projects as a way of establishing management practices.

Social entrepreneurship requires an active interpretation in order to be managed in practice. Both natural and artificial capital influence social entrepreneurship in sport. Natural capital refers to the location, climate, accessibility and natural surroundings of a sports organization. Some sports organizations, such as professional teams, relocate to certain locations due to the population density. This often occurs with teams in sports such as ice hockey in the United States moving to southern states due to migration patterns. These sport teams originated in cold weather climates but moved to warmer climates because of a need from fans to have sport teams in these regions. In addition, there has been competition from local governments to have a sport team as a way of attracting residents but also for reputation effects. This has meant the natural geography of a region is irrelevant when artificial playing fields can be built. Moreover, there are accessibility issues that impact sport teams, such as having appropriate transport methods for getting to sport stadiums. Nature sports such as surfing or rock climbing require distinct geographical conditions that might influence their location. However, artificial wave pools and indoor climbing venues have been introduced in areas that do not have the right natural conditions.

Artificial capital refers to the social structures influencing a sports organization. This differs in variety and magnitude depending on the cultural environment of a sports organization. The age and history of a region can influence the types of sport played. For example, sports such as cricket are popular in current and former Commonwealth countries due to the influence of the United Kingdom. Other sports such as judo and karate have been linked to the culture in countries such as Japan. Thus, certain sports are linked to the cultural heritage of a region and play an important role in the social development of an area. In the United States, sports such as football are linked to colleges and universities as a way of maintaining the alumni connection.

There is a need for sports organizations to develop measures for social entrepreneurship to assess its usefulness and potential. This will enable an assessment of the value derived from social entrepreneurship. Sports organizations are viewing social entrepreneurship as an asset that, when harnessed properly, can continue to provide benefits for years to come. Social enterprises can be classified based on economic and social criteria. There are four main dimensions related to economic criteria: (1) continuous activity, (2) autonomy, (3) economic risk and (4) paid work (Rinkinen et al., 2016). Continuous activity involves constantly producing a service or product that has a social purpose. Unlike non-profit organizations the difference with social enterprises is that a financial outcome is required. Autonomy relates to the social enterprise being self-sufficient and not dependent on other forms of funding. This independence means it is not managed by a government organization and maintains a focus on its business purpose. This is important in differentiating social enterprises from charities that are financed by donations.

Economic risk means that monetary outcomes are required and impact on the level of financial resources. In the early stages of a social enterprise it can take some time for profits to emerge. Thus, the financial viability of a social enterprise depends on the cashflow and profitability. Paid work means that the social enterprise acts like a regular business in paying employees. It can also use volunteers but the majority of its workers are on a salary. In response to the increased interest in social equity and empowerment, more initiatives around social entrepreneurship have been created. These solutions focus on the positive impacts coming from sport. In order to encourage more individuals in sport to be involved with social entrepreneurship both direct and indirect impression management techniques can be used.

In a seminal book, Goffman (1959) drew a link between social lives and theatre productions. This analogy to theatre is useful in impression management in terms of linking performance to actions and the behind the scenes preparatory work that is needed. There are two main components to impression management: motivation and construction (Leary and Kowalski, 1990). People are motivated to maintain an impression because of certain consequences that might affect their livelihoods. This means focusing on good things they do and telling others about this activity. Once this impression has been constructed then it is the person's responsibility to ensure it is maintained. Bolino et al. (2008:1080) define impression management as "efforts by an actor to create, maintain, protect or otherwise alter an image held by a target audience." The audience differs depending on the context and intention of the actor. Some audiences are static but others are dynamic and change depending on the situation.

Schneider (1981:25) stated that impression management was "an attempt by one person (actor) to affect the perceptions of her or him by another person (target)." This means influencing how others view your actions. This is important in maintaining the credibility of an individual in terms of how they are perceived by others. Another definition by Tedeschi and Reiss (1981:3) defines impression management as "any behaviour by a person that has the purpose of controlling or manipulating the attributions and impressions formed of that person by others." Impression management involves entities having ideas about how they are viewed and perceived by others. This means that impression management can be used as a way to highlight how social entrepreneurship is a new model of entrepreneurship that is based on the idea that business ventures should have a social purpose. Thus, sports organizations can use impression management as a way of marketing their social enterprises. These are stated in Table 3.4 below.

Social innovation

Social innovation is defined as "any new program, product, idea or initiative that changes a basic routine, a resource or authority flow, in addition to the norms,

TABLE 3.4 Impression management techniques for sport social enterprises

Technique	Example
Direct techniques – Assertive	
Ingratiation	Flattering athletes to act as social entrepreneur role models.
Intimidation	Pushing athletes into social entrepreneurship as part of their work for a sports club.
Promotion	Marketing social entrepreneurship endeavors linked to a sports club.
Exemplification	Going beyond normal duties to engage in social entrepreneurship.
Supplication	Being dependent on social enterprises for money.
Defensive	
Accounts	Providing explanations for being a social entrepreneur.
Disclaimers	Explanations that lessen risks.
Apologies	Being responsible for events through engaging in social entrepreneurship.
Prosocial behavior	Behaviors that include social entrepreneurship.
Indirect techniques – Assertive	
Boasting	Telling others about social entrepreneurship.
Blaring	Limiting connections to disadvantaged enterprises.
Burnishing	Focusing on the positive aspects of social enterprises.
Blasting	Exaggerating a social enterprise.
Defensive	
Burying	Hiding unfavorable social enterprises.
Blurring	Combining different social enterprises in order to conceal negative occurrences.
Boosting	Subsidizing a failing social venture with another project.
Belittling	Focusing on the negative attributes of a social venture.

Adapted from Brandon-Lai et al. (2016)

values or beliefs of a social system, while having durability and impact across different scales" (Moore et al., 2012:185). This lengthy definition of social innovation takes a broad approach to change by including a need for systemic cultural shifts that are different to what is currently being done. Emphasizing a systems approach highlights the way social issues need to be resolved in a holistic manner.

The concept of social innovation has changed from being a centralized government-led initiative to being a local community-led need. This has resulted in customized solutions being developed that relate to a specific niche in the community. This new ideology in social innovation research has resulted in a multi-stakeholder approach to social innovation. Thereby, instead of a dictatorial approach a more cross-sectorial approach is taken to solve social problems. Noack and Federwisch (2019) suggest that social innovation can be defined through three elements; "(1) the satisfaction of unfulfilled social needs, (2) the empowerment of marginalized and socially excluded groups and (3) the construction and alternation of network relationships." This definition encapsulates a view of social innovation originating from reconfigurations of social problems. This means social issues are solved differently based on intentional and unintentional outcomes from the innovation process.

There are numerous external factors that influence social innovation including the political, economic, social and technological environment (Noack and Federwisch, 2019). Political factors include the agendas and discourses involved in sport policy. Increasingly, policies regarding sport are being used for a number of concerns including the building of healthy communities. There are four different ways of socio-technical transition; these are reorientation, endogenous renewal, emergent transformation and purposive transformation. The reorientation way means changing the current direction of innovation to focus on new needs. This involves coordinating the flow of resources into endeavors that are likely to be more successful. Endogenous renewal means changing the internal resources into something more valuable. This requires a high level of coordination and project management.

Place is an important part of entrepreneurship studies as they provide the physical and social conditions for activity to take place. Places are differentiated by the way they are built and how resources are politically mobilized. People have various opinions about places due to their experiences and involvement. These perceptions are influenced by the market and regulatory forces that interact in the environment. Designing places better can facilitate economic and social processes that are conducive to entrepreneurship. Table 3.5 below states some ways to facilitate social innovation in sport places.

Fitness industry

The fitness industry is a good example of a sports industry that has substantially changed as a result of entrepreneurial activities. As Woolf (2008:53) states "in the past decades, health and fitness clubs have gone from weight training facilities to resort style facilities offering services as varied as cardiovascular fitness programs, beauty treatments, and full service restaurants." This has required fitness managers to think in an entrepreneurial manner in order to be competitive. Fitness clubs can be analyzed through services including professional, consumer, peripheral, facilities and secondary (Chelladurai et al., 1987). Professional services include training and development. There are now more personal trainers at fitness clubs that tailor services to suit individual members. Consumer's services are

TABLE 3.5 Ways to facilitate social innovation in sport places

Type	Examples
Context	
Building local assets	Encouraging social entrepreneurship in local sports clubs.
Continued prioritization	Placing social entrepreneurship at the forefront of sport discussions.
Dedicated institutionalization	Creating sport social enterprises.
Sustained funding	Obtaining finance from sports clubs for social ventures.

Adapted from Pancholi et al. (2019)

mass-market services such as aerobic classes and the use of gymnasiums. There has been an increase in fitness clubs that are open 24 hours a day to suit the changing lifestyle trends of individuals. In addition, different types of consumer services are needed, such as yoga, swimming and other types of sport. Peripheral services include those related to core fitness activity such as clothing and psychotherapists. Facilities and equipment range in size and cost depending on the type of fitness club. New sports such as pilates require different kinds of equipment that may be costly for fitness clubs to hire or buy. Equipment might be related to gender and age so it needs to suit the demographics of customers at the fitness clubs. Secondary services include naturopaths and dieticians who can be used in conjunction with the core services.

There are diverse services that fitness clubs offer including group activities, counseling, competitions, childcare and food services. The main service dimensions of fitness clubs involve changes in physical, mental or pleasure levels (Lagrosen and Lagrosen, 2007). Physical levels mean changes in appearance that can be analyzed through weight and height measurements. Mental levels involve changes in mood or behavior that are linked to a physical activity. Pleasure levels are defined as how much enjoyment an individual receives from engaging in physical activity. These service dimensions can be measured through the quality of fitness services and this includes service quality, management commitment to service quality, programming, personal interaction, task interaction, other clients, service failure, service recovery and perceived service quality (Chang and Chelladurai, 2003). The service climate involves the overall perception of how a fitness club is operating and involves whether people are happy about the level of service. The managers and owners of fitness clubs need to be committed to constantly upgrading and listening to members' concerns. Programming means the way people behave at fitness clubs and can vary by geographic area or level of intensity. Personal interaction differs in fitness clubs depending on how much individual support and advice members require. Some fitness club members prefer anonymity and privacy whilst others like more individual attention. Task interaction involves how much teaching is needed to master new classes. In the virtual start-up or beginning stages of a new class there might be a high level of mentorship or guidance needed. "Other clients" refers to individuals apart from fitness club members who use the same space. Some fitness clubs share their physical space with other businesses. Service failure involves disappointment or complaints about things that are not working properly. To ensure this does not happen a process of service recovery is required. This involves finding out what is wrong or incorrect and then obtaining a solution. The instances of service recovery will depend on the perceived service quality of the fitness club based on a range of factors including the level of services.

Conclusion

In this chapter I proposed a new way of thinking about social entrepreneurship by proposing a comprehensive overview that is tailored to the sports industry. This enables a multilevel approach to develop that highlights the dimensions applicable in sport. This new definition of social entrepreneurship integrates previous ones but is differentiated by the focus on sport. This is crucial as there are behavioral dimensions of social entrepreneurship evident in sport that recognize the uniqueness of the sports industry. This helps explore the social connectedness that many sports organizations have based on their internal and external networking capabilities.

This chapter discussed the processes and mechanisms for social entrepreneurship. A step-by-step approach to understanding how sports organizations can embed social entrepreneurship in their operations was stated. This involved focusing on how, for many individuals interested in sport, there is a lifestyle component to social entrepreneurship. This is due to social issues being part of an individual's life and interest in sport activities. The fitness industry was utilized as a way of understanding the process of entrepreneurship in terms of its effect on service quality.

References

Agnihotri, A. (2015) "Low-cost innovation in emerging markets," *Journal of Strategic Marketing*, 23(5): 399–411.

Alonso, A. and Bressan, A. (2016) "A resource-based view of the firm and micro and small Italian wine firms," *Journal of Wine Business Research*, 28(4): 349–368.

Ashraf, M., Razzaque, M. A., Liaw, S. T., Ray, P. K. and Hasan, M. R. (2019) "Social business as an entrepreneurship model in emerging economy: Systematic review and case study," *Management Decision*, 57(5): 1145–1161.

Atuahene-Gima, K. and Wei, Y. (2011) "The vital role of problem solving competence in new product success," *Journal of Product Innovation Management*, 28(1): 81–98.

Baden-Fuller, C. and Haefliger, S. (2013) "Business models and technological innovation," *Long Range Planning*, 46(6): 419–426.

Bolino, M., Kacmar, K., Turnley, W. and Gilstrap, J. (2008) "A multi-level review of impression management motives and behaviours," *Journal of Management*, 34(6): 1080–1109.

Brandon-Lai, B., Armstrong, C. and Ferris, G. (2016) "Organizational impression congruence: A conceptual model of multi-level impression management operation in sports science organisations," *Sport Management Review*, 19: 492–505.

Brockner, J., Higgins, T. and Low, M. (2004) "Regulatory focus theory and the entrepreneurial process," *Journal of Business Venturing*, 19: 203–220.

Chang, K. and Chelladurai, P. (2003) "System-based quality dimensions in fitness services: Development of the scale of quality," *The Service Industries Journal*, 23(5): 65–83.

Chelladurai, P., Scott, F. L. and Haywood-Farmer, J. (1987) "Dimensions of fitness services: Development of a model," *Journal of Sport Management*, 1(2): 159–172.

Costa, C. (2005) "The status and future of sport management: A delphi study," *Journal of Sport Management*, 19: 117–142.

D'Antone, S., Canning, L., Franklin-Johnson, E. and Spencer, R. (2017) "Concerned innovation: The ebb and flow between market and society," *Industrial Marketing Management*, 64, 66–78.

Davenport, T. and Prusak, L. (1998) *Working knowledge: How organisations manage what they know*. Boston, MA: Harvard Business School Press.

Dawson, D., Fountain, J. and Cohen, D. (2011) "Seasonality and the lifestyle 'conundrum': An analysis of lifestyle entrepreneurship in wine tourism regions," *Asia Pacific Journal of Tourism Research*, 16(5): 551–572.

Dennissen, M., Benschop, Y. and van den Brink, M. (2019) "Rethinking diversity management: An intersectional analysis of diversity networks," *Organization Studies*, in press.

Douglas, E. and Prentice, C. (2019) "Innovation and profit motivations for social entrepreneurship: A fuzzy-set analysis," *Journal of Business Research*, 99: 69–79.

Dyllick, T. and Hockerts, K. (2002) "Beyond the business case for corporate sustainability," *Business Strategy and the Environment*, 11(2): 130–141.

Edwards, M. and Rowe, K. (2019) "Managing sport for health: An introduction to the special issue," *Sport Management Review*, 22(1): 1–4.

Fedele, A. and Miniac, R. (2010) "Do social enterprises finance their investments differently from non-profit firms? The case of social residential services in Italy," *Journal of Social Entrepreneurship*, 1(2): 174–189.

Foss, N. and Saebi, T. (2017) "Fifteen years of research on business model innovation: How far have we come, and where should we go?" *Journal of Management*, 43(1): 200–227.

Geiger, S., Harrison, D., Kjellberg, H. and Mallard, A. (eds) (2014) "Being concerned about markets," *Concerned markets: Economic ordering for multiple values*, 1–18. Cheltenham: Edward Elgar.

Gërguri-Rashiti, S., Ramadani, V., Abazi-Alili, H., Dana, L. P. and Ratten, V. (2017) "ICT, innovation and firm performance: The transition economies context," *Thunderbird International Business Review*, 59(1): 93–102.

Godbey, G., Caldwell, L., Floyd, M. and Payne, L. (2005) "Contributions of leisure studies and recreation and park management research to the active living agenda," *American Journal of Preventative Medicine*, 28: 150–157.

Goffman, E. (1959) *The presentation of self in everyday life*. Garden City, NY: Doubleday.

Goulding, P., Baum, T. and Morrison, A. (2005) "Seasonal trading and lifestyle motivation," *Journal of Quality Assurance in Hospitality and Tourism*, 5(2–4): 209–238.

Hansmann, H. (1980) "The role of non-profit enterprise," *Yale Law Journal*, 89(5): 835–901.

Hudson, J., Males, J. and Kerr, J. (2019) "Introducing a basis psychological performance demand model for sport and organisations," *Coaching: An International Journal of Theory, Research and Practice*, in press, 1–15.

Jones, P., Jones, A., Williams-Burnett, N. and Ratten, V. (2017) "Let's get physical: Stories of entrepreneurial activity from sports coaches/instructors," *The International Journal of Entrepreneurship and Innovation*, 18(4): 219–230.

Jones, P., Klapper, R., Ratten, V. and Fayolle, A. (2018) "Emerging themes in entrepreneurial behaviours, identities and contexts," *The International Journal of Entrepreneurship and Innovation*, 19(4): 233–236.

Kalantaridis, C. and Bika, Z. (2006) "Local embeddedness and rural entrepreneurship: Case-study evidence from Cumbria, England," *Environment and Planning A*, 38: 1561–1579.

Kim, M. and James, J. (2016) "The theory of planned behaviours and intention of purchase sport team licensed merchandise," *Sport, Business and Management: An International Journal*, 6(2): 228–243.

Kim, Y. and Lui, S. (2015) "The impacts of external network and business group on innovation: Do the types of innovation matter?" *Journal of Business Research*, 68: 1964–1973.

Kim, W. and Mauborgne, R. (2005) "Value, innovation: A leap into the blue ocean," *Journal of Business Strategy*, 26: 22–28.

Kirby, D. (2004) "Entrepreneurship education: Can business schools meet the challenge?" *Education & Training*, 46(8/9): 510–519.

Klyver, K. and Foley, D. (2012) "Networking and culture in entrepreneurship," *Entrepreneurship & Regional Development*, 24(7–8): 561–588.

Knight, F. H. (1921) *Risk, uncertainty and profit*. Chicago, IL: University of Chicago Press.

Lagrosen, S. and Lagrosen, Y. (2007) "Exploring service quality in the health and fitness industry," *Managing Service Quality*, 17(1): 41–53.

Leary, M. and Kowalski, R. (1990) "Impression management: A literature review and two component mode," *Psychological Bulletin*, 107(1): 34–37.

Lusch, R. and Vargo, S. (2014) *Service dominant logic: Premises, perspectives, possibilities*. Cambridge: Cambridge University Press.

Marchant, B. and Mottiar, Z. (2011) "Understanding lifestyle entrepreneurs and digging beneath the issue of profits: Profiling surf tourism lifestyle entrepreneurs in Ireland," *Tourism Planning & Development*, 8(2): 171–183.

Marcketti, S., Niehm, L. and Fuloria, R. (2006) "An exploratory study of lifestyle entrepreneurship and its relationship to life quality," *Family and Consumer Sciences Research Journal*, 34: 241–259.

Martin, R. and Sunley, P. (2015) "On the notion of regional economic resilience: Conceptualization and explanation," *Journal of Economic Geography*, 15: 1–42.

Miloch, K. S., Lee, J., Kraft, P. M. and Ratten, V. (2012) "Click clack: Examining the strategic and entrepreneurial brand vision of Under Armour," *International Journal of Entrepreneurial Venturing*, 4(1): 42–57.

Moore, M., Westley, F. and Broadhead, T. (2012) "Social finance intermediaries and social innovation," *Journal of Social Entrepreneurship*, 3(2): 184–205.

Murphy, P. J. and Coombes, S. M. (2009) "A model of social entrepreneurial discovery," *Journal of Business Ethics*, 87(3): 325–336.

Neesson, P., Caniels, M.,Vos, B. and de Jong, J. (2018) "The intrapreneurial employee: Toward a integrated model of intrapreneurship and research agenda," *International Entrepreneurship and Management Journal*, 15(2): 545–571.

Noack, A. and Federwisch, T. (2019) "Social innovation in rural regions: Urban impulses and cross-border constellations of actors," *Sociologia Ruralis*, 59(1): 92–112.

Osterwalder, A. and Pigneur, Y. (2010) *Business model generation: A handbook for visionaries, game changers and challengers*. New York: Wiley.

Pancholi, S., Yigitcanlar, T. and Guaralda, M. (2019) "Place making for innovation and knowledge intensive activities: The Australian experience," *Technological Forecasting and Social Change*, in press.

Philipson, S. (2016) "Radical innovation of a business model: Is business modelling a key to understand the essence of doing business?" *Competitiveness Review*, 26(2): 132–146.

Potts, J. and Ratten, V. (2016) "Sports innovation: Introduction to the special section," *Innovation*, 18(3): 233–237.

Ratten, V. (2009) "Adoption of technological innovations in the m-commerce industry," *International Journal of Technology Marketing*, 4(4): 355–367.

Ratten, V. (2011) "Practical implications and future research directions for international sports management," *Thunderbird International Business Review*, 53(6): 763–770.

Ratten, V. (2012) "Sport entrepreneurship: Challenges and directions for future research," *International Journal of Entrepreneurial Venturing*, 4(1): 65–76.

Ratten, V. (2014) "Future research directions for collective entrepreneurship in developing countries: A small and medium-sized enterprise perspective," *International Journal of Entrepreneurship and Small Business*, 22(2): 266–274.

Ratten, V. (2015) "Athletes as entrepreneurs: The role of social capital and leadership ability," *International Journal of Entrepreneurship and Small Business*, 25(4): 442–455.

Ratten, V. (2018a) "Entrepreneurial intentions of surf tourists," *Tourism Review*, 73(2): 262–276.

Ratten, V. (2018b) *Sport entrepreneurship: Developing and sustaining an entrepreneurial sports culture.* Heidelberg: Springer.

Ratten, V. and Ferreira, J. J. (eds) (2016) *Sport entrepreneurship and innovation.* London: Taylor & Francis.

Rinkinen, S., Oikarinen, T. and Melkas, H. (2016) "Social enterprises in regional innovation systems: A review of Finnish regional strategies," *European Planning Studies*, 24(4): 723–741.

Schneider, D. (1981) "Tactical self-presentations: Toward a broader conception," in J. Tedeschi (ed.), *Impression management theory and social psychological research*, pp. 23–40. New York: Academic Press.

Stephan, V., Patterson, M., Kelly, C. and Mair, J. (2016) "Organizations driving positive social change: A review and an integrative framework of change processes," *Journal of Management*, 42(5): 1250–1281.

Tedeschi, K. and Reiss, M. (1981) "Predicaments and verbal tactics of impression management," in C. Antaki (ed.), *Ordinary language explanations of social behaviour.* London: Academic Press.

Teece, D. (2010) "Business models, business strategy and innovation," *Long Range Planning*, 43(2/3): 172–194.

Vamplew, W. (2019) "The commodification of sport: Exploring the nature of the sports product," *The International Journal of the History of Sport*, in press.

Woolf, J. (2008) "Competitive advantage in the health and fitness industry: Developing service bundles," *Sport Management Review*, 11: 51–75.

Yang, X. and Andersson, D. E. (2018) "Spatial aspects of entrepreneurship and innovation," *The Annals of Regional Science*, 61(3): 457–462.

Yeh, S. S., Ma, T. and Huan, T. C. (2016) "Building social entrepreneurship for the hotel industry by promoting environmental education," *International Journal of Contemporary Hospitality Management*, 28(6): 1204–1224.

Zeimers, G., Anagnostopoulos, C., Zintz, T. and Willem, A. (2019) "Organizational learning for corporate social responsibility in sport organizations," *European Sport Management Quarterly*, 19(1): 80–101.

4

ENTREPRENEURIAL ECOSYSTEMS IN SPORT

Introduction

Entrepreneurship does not occur in isolation but is the result of multiple factors (Bui et al., 2018). It can be planned but it is also the result of serendipity. This makes a holistic approach to studying entrepreneurship important as it acknowledges the myriad ways that innovation is developed (Audretsch and Belitski, 2017). Complexity science is a way to study and understand entrepreneurship as it focuses on the unpredictable patterns of behavior (Roundy et al., 2018). Entrepreneurship in sport is based on novel interactions in society and provides a way to understand the connections amongst entities in a region. These interactions form part of an entrepreneurial ecosystem and are based on the capacity of entities to change. This is a complex process as it can follow a non-linear path that is based on a set of interactions.

A useful way of measuring the impact of social entrepreneurship in sport is by focusing on the interactions amongst actors in an ecosystem. To do this the helix model for innovation can be used as it focuses on collaboration between universities, industry and government. Originally this helix model was called the triple helix but was expanded to a fourth helix by introducing civil society then a fifth helix by acknowledging the role of the natural environment. The interactions amongst these helix variables form part of the entrepreneurial ecosystem for the sports industry.

In this chapter, I extend previous research on entrepreneurial ecosystems on helix systems to a sport context. Despite the importance of collaboration in entrepreneurship, there have been few studies that have focused on sport as the platform that drives entrepreneurship. Part of this interaction is based on social entrepreneurs bridging the gap between profit and non-profit motives to incorporate new business ideas into the market. This chapter will outline a new conceptual link between sport and social entrepreneurship by focusing on entrepreneurial ecosystems.

This chapter is structured as follows. First, the role of communities in encouraging sport-based entrepreneurial ecosystems is stated as a way to integrate multiple stakeholders. The co-development process for creating social forms of sport entrepreneurship is then discussed, which highlights the need to explore new possibilities in the marketplace. Next, the building of social capital in sport is examined as a way of building more knowledge communities.

Alertness and entrepreneurial opportunities

Sports organizations need to be alert to entrepreneurial opportunities regarding social issues by taking into account their environment. Kirzner (1979:48) defined the concept of alertness in evaluating opportunities as an "ability to notice, without search, opportunities that have hitherto been overlooked." Being alert to new possibilities is crucial for social entrepreneurs in sport who need to stay ahead of the marketplace and remain competitive. The capability to be alert is a skill that entrepreneurs have by their very nature of being forward-thinking individuals (Estevao et al., 2017). The concept of alertness in entrepreneurial activities has three main behavioral components: (1) scanning and searching for new information, (2) sorting disparate information and (3) evaluating the potential of information (Tang et al., 2012). Entrepreneurial alertness has more of an innovation focus and is defined as "a cognitive resource that affords the entrepreneur a cognitive capacity to identify opportunities, ahead of others" (Adomako et al., 2018:4). Alert entrepreneurs use their social networking capability to mobilize resources, which is important to the growth of the sports industry. The ability to harness resources within a social network structure is a way to capitalize on opportunities. By leveraging the connections in a social network, alert entrepreneurs are able to explore new possibilities (Ratten, 2004). Part of this process is focusing on social peers who create the resources within a network. To utilize these resources a social networking approach is needed to assemble the requisite resources for a particular need. In order to have the desired outcome there needs to be concurrent interaction amongst network members.

Entrepreneurial alertness can be analyzed by focusing on the different types of discourse used to analyze entrepreneurship, which are: social, ecological, business, emotive and aesthetic (Poldner et al., 2017). Social discourse involves interactions with other individuals that encourage information sharing. Depending on the context, the social discourse can include different types of stakeholders such as businesses, community groups and government entities (Ratten, 2017). The process of social discourse involves auditing, affiliating and accommodating others (Poldner et al., 2017). Auditing means listening and understanding another's point of view based on their experiences. This can take some time to do as it requires a thorough examination of previous experiences. Affiliating means bringing together individuals based on common characteristics or behavior. Different kinds of affiliations can include sport teams or geographic regions (Welty Peachey et al., 2018). Accommodating means accepting viewpoints when they are different to your own. This means being tolerant of socio-cultural differences that can often lead to misunderstandings (Ratten and Tajeddini, 2018). Ecological discourse involves understanding how "entrepreneurs interact with natural resources such as plants, water and air, as well as with animals" (Poldner et al., 2017:232). Increasingly the environment is of a concern to entrepreneurs due to the emphasis on sustainability. Business discourse involves analyzing financial trends about potential business opportunities. This is an important way to learn market knowledge that might bring about good fortune. Emotive discourse is about feelings and the associated physiological changes. Good performance outcomes can be linked to an associated happy state, which can affect other individuals. Aesthetic discourse involves the materials and colors used to make products or services. Sometimes inventions have different aesthetics that distinguish them in the marketplace.

Inventions are ideas that represent breakthrough changes in society whilst innovations are further developments based on initial inventions (Hjalager, 2002). Inventions normally involve a scientific idea that is game-shifting and causes existing practices to become obsolete. The reality is that most sport inventions need to be progressed from the initial concept to a commercially viable product or services. Increasingly, sport inventions are inspired by ideas in other industries. To transfer knowledge there needs to be consideration about the infrastructural, regulation, technological and trade system (Hjalager, 2002). The infrastructural system includes the essential services needed from an industry in order to function properly. This includes roads, airports and Internet connectivity. In the sports industry there are arenas and other venues that are cultural attractions. In addition, there are natural sport venues such as beaches and parks that are needed to play sport. Thus, when assessing the knowledge needed to transform an area into a sporting precinct there should be a focus on traffic and transport to the venues. The regulatory system involves the safety and precautions needed to play sport. This includes the use of equipment and referees in games. In addition, economic controls such as ticket prices and hourly wages may be needed. The technological system is increasingly relevant for the sports industry that uses online communication to broadcast games. However, technology can also come in the form of production and manufacturing. The trade system involves the certifications and approvals of sporting bodies needed to play sport. All these different types of systems are required to make an entrepreneurial ecosystem function properly.

Entrepreneurial ecosystems

Faced with the increasing demands of the competitive global sport market, sports organizations are focusing on entrepreneurship as a way to resolve social problems. To do this, collaboration through being a member of an entrepreneurial ecosystem is used to create a more proactive culture. Trust amongst team members of an ecosystem is a notable determinant in finding ways to be involved in social entrepreneurship. The concept of entrepreneurial ecosystems derives from the research on entrepreneurial systems, which is important but seldom used anymore. Spilling

(1996:91) defined entrepreneurial systems as consisting of "a complexity and diversity of actors, roles and environmental factors that interact to determine the entrepreneurial performance of a region or locality." The difference between entrepreneurial systems and ecosystems is that the ecosystem implies a concurrent feedback process that continually evolves whilst entrepreneurial systems refer to more one-way interactions. However, the concepts are very similar but the increased usage of the word "ecosystem" might be due to environmental factors becoming more important in entrepreneurship research. For this reason, it is better to use the terminology "ecosystem" as it implies relationships amongst entities that act in a way that is similar to real life.

Entrepreneurial ecosystems can be considered as comprising a set of ingredients that are needed to make a recipe (Malecki, 2018). This interesting metaphor means that when the right ingredients are combined then there will be the desired outcome. Entrepreneurial ecosystems need some ingredients more than others and the mixture of these ingredients will affect what is made (Yang and Andersson, 2018). Sports organizations in an ecosystem need the support of the government and citizens in order to facilitate social roles in society (Ratten, 2010). Sport entrepreneurial ecosystems face obstacles if they do not receive help in the form of supportive policies and programs. Thus, stadiums and other venues for sport are needed to create appropriate entrepreneurial ecosystems.

Each entrepreneurial ecosystem differs in terms of its attributes, objectives and processes (Miles and Morrison, 2018). This means every entrepreneurial ecosystem needs to be analyzed in terms of its network of actors and context. Unlike other types of ecosystems the emphasis in entrepreneurial ones is on the complex adaptive systems that can create some confusion. This means the elements constituting an entrepreneurial ecosystem will be geographically bounded but also reliant on cultural and societal elements. In thriving sport-based entrepreneurial ecosystems there is a continual flux of change brought about by dynamic interactions in society. This is important, as the sports industry has moved to a more knowledge economy where new ideas are needed to identify opportunities that can be commercialized.

Entrepreneurial ecosystems are the result of dynamic interactions between individuals in a society that result in creative ideas (Acs et al., 2014). The ability of individuals to be entrepreneurial is based on their attitudes and aspirations to act in an innovative and proactive manner. Entrepreneurship is a result of context, which can be referred to as the cultural, economic and social conditions of a place. The opportunities available to entrepreneurs will depend on contextual factors that are influenced by public and private entities. The character of a place is based on the types of individuals and businesses that reside there. Places that have an entrepreneurial spirit tend to evolve better when new businesses are created from innovative ideas. This results in a place having a competitive advantage because entrepreneurship is at the center of the system. It helps a place to have an entrepreneurial culture that values collaboration and shares information. Appropriate infrastructure is needed in a place in order to facilitate both the emergence of new businesses and entrepreneurship. Entrepreneurial ecosystems are environments that encompass a distinct geographic or digital space and can vary in size and magnitude. This means that ecosystems are shaped by economic conditions that benefit from interdependent relationships. By facilitating mutual engagements, entities in an ecosystem coexist.

Entrepreneurial ecosystems consist of different elements, such as customers, capital markets and culture, which interact with each other (Isenberg, 2010). The connectivity in an ecosystem depends on the type of leadership, institutions and amenities existing in a place. This means that the norms of behavior will have a significant effect on entrepreneurial behavior. The term "ecosystem" can mean a range of things depending on the context but mostly refers to the social structures and relationships existing in a physical or digital space (Neumeyer and Corbett, 2017). In a social entrepreneurial ecosystem there is a reliance on community development, support staff, volunteers, businesses and mentors. This is shown in Table 4.1 below.

Some sport social entrepreneurial ecosystems are based on service systems. Service ecosystems are defined as "relatively self-contained self-adjusting system(s) of resource integrating actors connected by shared institutional logics and mutual value creation through service exchange" (Lusch and Vargo, 2014:161). Sport service ecosystems are particularly relevant due to the role of volunteers and fans, which is unlike other industries. In the past, the production of sport services was done by firms with little interaction with consumers. This has changed with consumers acting as co-creators of value and being more involved in the service experience. Thus, the separation between production and consumption has narrowed. More market relationships are being formed in sport that take a co-creation view and service ecosystems are part of this process. Instead of consumers being end users they are now viewed as co-creators and play a dynamic role in facilitating entrepreneurship. The participation of consumers as users of sport services provides a more current view of what is occurring in the sports industry. Part of this participation involves the use of social networks to transmit and receive knowledge about potential social entrepreneurship ideas.

TABLE 4.1 Contributions to sport social entrepreneurial ecosystems

Contributor	Supporting activity
Community development staff	Entrepreneurial networks
	Social legitimacy
Support staff	Business modeling
	Accounting and finance
Volunteers	Time and resource allocation
	Community collaboration
Businesses	Advocacy and incentives
	Technology advice
Mentors	Banking relationships
	Regional grants and funds

Social networks

Network theory has been used by Stangler and Bell-Masterson (2015) to explain entrepreneurial ecosystems in terms of connectivity, density, diversity and fluidity. Cohen (2006) suggests that the main components of an ecosystem are the informal network, formal network, university, government, professional and support services, capital services and talent pool. Social networks are an important part of entrepreneurial ecosystems (Neumeyer et al., 2018). Both formal and informal networks are used in entrepreneurial ecosystems as a way to facilitate interaction. Networks provide a source of information and knowledge that can enable entrepreneurship. As a key system component of ecosystems, networks enable ideas to emerge (Isenberg, 2010). Networks can be considered as social ties or bonding social capital that enables communication amongst disparate entities (Light and Dana, 2013). Strong ties occur in networks when there is frequent interaction and a sense of mutual goals, whilst weak ties involve infrequent interaction. Networks enable entities to be more integrated into social systems. Formal networks include those found in organizations, which meet on a set basis. They can include professional services, government agencies and research institutions. Informal networks occur in a more ad hoc and sporadic manner and tend to be unplanned.

There are three main types of networks in social capital: bonding, bridging and linking (Zhou and Kaplanidou, 2018). Bonding refers to network members that share similar traits or identities. Through repeat interaction individuals gain a sense of familiarity that enables trust to develop. This is important in helping create a sense of solidarity through social discourse. Sociability is part of this interaction as it enables individuals to communicate about events. Bridging refers to individuals who have to work together for a shared reason. This means bringing together people who would otherwise not see any reason for interaction. Bridging can help foster creativity as diverse points of view are taken into account to provide a sense of mutual understanding. This tolerance for others is important in establishing community inclusiveness. Linking involves reaching out to others for specific needs. This can empower others to come together for a shared purpose. The density of social networks is important within the context of sport as it relates to the quality and frequency of information exchanged. Network density can be sparse or dense depending on the intensity and formality of the interaction. Sparse networks are configured in such a way that the relations with actors are not often connected and only used for specific functions (Sorensen, 2007). Dense networks on the other hand include multiple relations with actors who frequently interact. These networks provide the basis for social networks and help determine how to manage stakeholders.

Stakeholder management

There is growing acceptance that the increase in the social economy has been made due to changes in the way business operates. This has made social changes not happen without innovation. The challenge for sports organizations is to develop social innovation strategies that consider the needs of stakeholders. This is required in order to respond to social pressures and the expectations of society. Stakeholder management is a way to enhance the competitiveness of sports organizations by being a source of innovation. Through social innovation there can be increased efforts at changing sport practices. Structural stakeholder management leads to relationships being developed that are key to the enhancement of overall operations. This is different to processual stakeholder arrangements that emphasize knowledge and learning.

Stakeholders are defined in general terms as "any group or individual who can affect or is affected by the achievement of the organisation's objectives" (Freeman, 1984:46). Stakeholders influence the direction of sports organizations due to their input about future developments. Stakeholders can have a normative or instrumental influence on organizations (Ayuso et al., 2006). The normative view suggests that sport managers need to consider the view of stakeholders due to their mutual interests. This means stakeholders have a right to express their opinions in a way that shapes the development of sports organizations. The instrumental view holds the organization as the main decision maker who manages relationships with stakeholders. This means that rather than listening to the opinions of stakeholders a sports organization can make its own choices about its strategic decisions. In this way stakeholders have some degree of influence but are not the main consideration. The stakeholders' relationship with the sports organization depends on the level of interaction. In addition, the density of the stakeholder network will determine the level of legitimate interest. Some stakeholders will see their role as being more influential than others. This means the level of intrinsic value a stakeholder brings to a sports organization needs to be examined. Focusing on the need for a stakeholder can help determine the level of influence they have in a sports organization. Stakeholders, such as the government, who fund sport programs will likely have more influence but fans can also have a strong impact. The fans are likely to be a secondary consideration in terms of loyalty but also allegiance to the sports organization. This involves looking at fans as stakeholders who have ethical and moral rights.

Stakeholders can be classified into primary and secondary groups depending on the centrality of their relationship to an organization. Primary stakeholders are defined as "stakeholders who are essential for the business itself to exist and/or have some kind of formal contract with the business (owners, employees, customers and suppliers)" (Ayuso et al., 2006:476). These core stakeholders normally have the most input about potential changes in a sports organization. This includes the type and purpose of social ventures they may be involved in. Primary stakeholders are the easiest to pinpoint as they are involved in a close relationship with the sports organization. In some sports the owners may be answerable to a league or institution. In addition, the sport can be part of a franchise structure so the owner is common amongst a number of teams. Sports organizations listed on the stock exchange have shareholders as owners. Secondary stakeholders involved political and social groups that have a vested interest in an organization. This means they can influence a sports organization through the media or other public outlets. The credibility of a sports organization in society will depend on how well it considers the needs of secondary stakeholders. There are also peripheral stakeholders who are interested at different stages of the life of a sports organization. In times of success these peripheral stakeholders might show more interest if it reflects well on them. At other times they can be considered as fringe stakeholders as they are not clearly visible in discussions. This means it may be hard to identify fringe stakeholders because they can alternate between having a close and a distant relationship with a sports organization. A more useful way to assess stakeholders is by focusing on their interaction in the sport community.

Community interaction

Sports organizations dominate the local economic landscape of communities and have a capacity for social entrepreneurship. Sport and social activities often coexist in communities and as a consequence they are linked to entrepreneurial activities. Sport benefits communities in terms of sociocultural development and quality of life. Sports organizations often enjoy substantial local support in terms of both direct and indirect financial assistance. This can serve as a tool to stimulate community revitalization by using resources from both the public and private sectors. The two main views regarding the governance process of entrepreneurial ecosystems in communities are the bottom up and top down approach (Neumeyer et al., 2018). The bottom up approach suggests that ecosystems are a result of the natural evolution of a community that progresses with social change. As part of this approach it is considered normal that various stakeholders interact for business purposes. As part of the coordination process there is a set of norms and regulations that entities in the ecosystem adhere to. This creates a sense of balance and purpose amongst the various stakeholders in the ecosystem. There is no specific intention in the bottom-up approach to be entrepreneurial, rather it is by serendipity that things happen. On the other hand, the top–down approach has more formality as there is a deliberate plan to create an entrepreneurial ecosystem. This means having government policies and business support that encourages innovation. Strategically designing an ecosystem with an entrepreneurial flavor allows for more emphasis on certain industries. This is evident in sporting cities such as Melbourne in Australia having a number of sporting arenas in close proximity. In addition, Melbourne is the only city in the world that has a public holiday for a football final. Whilst the city might not have been specifically designed as a sporting city, an entrepreneurial ecosystem around sport has emerged due to the closeness of sports facilities to the central business district. This has meant a knowledge spillover effect between sport and business and helps to encourage not only a sport ecosystem but also sport ventures that support the needs of sport teams.

Prosocial attitudes involve providing social benefits to others that come from a sense of caring. This includes having empathy and compassion for others. The inherent synergies between sport and social entrepreneurship are not currently addressed in an appropriate way in entrepreneurial ecosystems. The topic of sport and social entrepreneurship remains a divergent theme in the literature with some exceptions. In order to alleviate some of the malaise coming from inequality in society, there needs to be more support for social entrepreneurship. Social entrepreneurship can be used as a form of preemptive action to influence change in the environment. Sport firms involved in social entrepreneurship seek new opportunities based on societal conditions. This means being willing to change and able to be strategically flexible in terms of the available social opportunities. To do this, firms need to transform their business processes by leveraging existing and new knowledge. This can alter social conditions by extending opportunities to undervalued parts of society. To distinguish social entrepreneurship from other forms of entrepreneurship there needs to be a stream of continuous innovation focused on social change. This can occur through entrepreneurship that has specific strategies in place to deal with social disruptions.

Strategic entrepreneurship involves "taking entrepreneurial actions with strategic perspective, or taking strategic action with an entrepreneurial mindset" (Mazzei, 2018:2). Integrating both the entrepreneurship and strategic management domains, strategic entrepreneurship represents an effort to explore new opportunities for sports organizations. Depending on a sports organization's entrepreneurial characteristics strategic entrepreneurship can be manifested in different ways. This depends on the firm's industry and what outcomes are needed from certain actions. To incorporate a strategic perspective into a sports organization's activities there needs to be a willingness to exploit current advantages in the marketplace. In management theories, a concept needs to be defined in terms of capturing its essential meaning, being parsimonious and avoiding tautology (Suddaby, 2010). This means a concept should have the appropriate characteristics and meaning that avoids repetition whilst providing a simplistic understanding.

Cooperatives

Cooperatives are a form of social entrepreneurship as they deploy social goals through collaborative activity. To be successful cooperatives need to have services that its members value. Cooperatives have diverse roles and they are normally conceptualized as being an association of people who jointly control an enterprise. This means there are shared goals about the required economic and social needs. People become members of a cooperative on a voluntary basis (Figueiredo and Franco, 2018). Cooperatives play a key role in the social economy as they combine both non-profit and social activities with financial objectives. This is due to the social economy emphasizing the role of people in the decision-making process of communities.

Cooperatives are a type of business structure that has existed for a long time but recently regained popularity in the marketplace. This is due to the emphasis on the sharing economy in terms of groups of people working together for a common goal. Cooperatives seem to be more resilient than other types of business organizations due to their ability to cross-subsidize members. This means in times of hardship members can receive help and this creates a sense of solidarity. This type of organizational structure is useful to study in terms of social entrepreneurship due to its cooperative processes.

The three main ways to assess cooperator satisfaction are by analyzing compatibility, partner selection and government policies (Figueiredo and Franco, 2018). Compatibility refers to how different stakeholders involved in social entrepreneurship feel about each other. When there is a mutual dependence then the compatibility is likely to be higher. This helps ensure partners work together on common social causes. Forming deep relationships can help foster trust and commitment between partners. This enables new ideas to be developed that can be facilitated through cooperation. More lasting relationships are likely to result when there is a common bond and reliance on others for sources of information. This means having sustainable relationships that enable different partnerships in social entrepreneurship to continue.

Partner selection means choosing the right people or organizations for a task. Having good selection criteria can help to find appropriate partners. This enables cooperative relationships to develop that encourage the sharing of ideas. Managing relationships properly can enable further cooperation in the future. This helps with ensuring partners stay loyal and reciprocate in times of need. To do this, social networks can be used as a way to facilitate better information networks.

Cooperatives enable the cultural needs of members to be pursued through collective means. This helps to build a sense of solidarity about future aspirations for members. Cooperatives are an umbrella term that can include a variety of different organizational forms. There are seven guiding principles for understanding cooperatives and these are known as the Rochdale principles (Quarter et al., 2001). These principles, which originated in one of the first cooperatives in England, are: (1) autonomy and independence, (2) concern for community, (3) cooperation, (4) democratic member control, (5) member economic participation, (6) training and information and (7) voluntary and open membership. Autonomy revolves around basing decisions on the input of members without having influence from other sources. This helps build a sense of independence and enables members to take the route they believe will give them the most joy. Concern for community means there is an emphasis on the well-being of members in terms of how they are coping. This is important as it brings a sense of belonging to members of a cooperative.

Democracy in terms of letting each member have a say is important in cooperatives and brings a sense of transparency to what is happening. Members can feel secure that there is an open process in voting rights. Cooperation is a feature of cooperatives as they depend on mutual interaction for success. This can occur in a number of ways such as through information dissemination or the sharing of resources. Individuals become members of a cooperative by giving

TABLE 4.2 Sport policy solutions for cooperatives

Type	Solution
Expectations	Have clear goals about the outcomes from social entrepreneurship.
	Be open about what is needed.
Learning	Facilitate dissemination of knowledge and information.
	Be proactive about acquiring new resources.
Network	Incorporate different stakeholders in the decision-making process.
	Facilitate co-creation of new ideas by involving multiple network members.
Protection	Safeguard ideas until they enter the market.
	Have procedures in place to nurture new ideas.
Stimulation	Encourage comments and feedback about ideas.
	Bring together people from different perspectives to challenge the status quo.
Upscaling	Develop innovation past the initial idea to bring about solutions to social problems.
	Build on existing ideas by taking new approaches.
Vision	Have a goal in mind for the social problem.
	Adjust the vision based on changing circumstances.

financial aid. This can be an inflow or outflow activity depending on whether the money is paid or received. Training is a way members can obtain new skills about technological developments. This is useful for competitiveness reasons. Voluntary and open membership means joining a cooperative is done by choice. In addition, members can leave at any time if they choose. In order to manage cooperatives there needs to be specific solutions to solve each different type. This is stated in Table 4.2 below.

Co-development process

Co-development is defined as "the joint development of new products with customers through interaction and participation at various stages of the new product development process" (Stock et al., 2017:201). According to boundary theory, companies should go outside their internal structures to access knowledge from other sources (Tushman, 1977). This enables information about ideas to be disseminated amongst a company's stakeholders. During the new product development process it is important to obtain knowledge from a variety of sources in order to proactively exchange ideas. Boundary theory is incorporated within the most recent theory on co-creation. Grönroos and Voima (2013) suggest co-development as a way to bridge the relationships between companies, customers and suppliers. This is useful in the dynamic sports industry that has a quick flow of information. Cooperative relationships are important, especially when time is of the essence and the use of multiple entities in the innovation process is required. In the past, the customer and company had an arm's length relationship but this has changed with more customers active in the idea stage. Resource dependency theory suggests that organizations need to acquire resources from their environment as part of the value creation process (Pfeffer and Salancik, 1978).

To enable trust there needs to be a focus on mutual benefits facilitated by sports organizations involved in social entrepreneurship. From the perspective of sport teams there are reputational benefits associated with social entrepreneurship. This means leaders need to be present in the conversation about how best to be involved in social entrepreneurship. This requires some trust to exist in terms of having confidence in the behavior of the members involved. Trust is defined as

> the willingness of a party to be vulnerable to the actions of another party based on the expectation that the other will perform a particular action important to the trustor, irrespective of the ability to monitor or control that other party.
>
> *Mayer et al., 1995:712*

To enable trust there should be open communication that facilitates the exchanging of information. Information that is market sensitive needs to be shared based on the integrity of the partners. This involves assessing the character of organizations based on their intentions and competence. Both inspirational motivation and intellectual stimulation can be used to encourage communication (Boies et al., 2015). Inspirational motivation involves focusing on the good things coming in the future from current actions. This may include examples of how collective action has benefitted organizations. Intellectual stimulation involves thinking in a different way and challenging the status quo. Creativity is part of having intellectual stimulation as it involves continually questioning the way things are done. As part of the co-development process, knowledge needs to be transferred effectively. Knowledge can take a variety of forms from economic development, market impact to public value. The advantages and disadvantages for each type are stated in Table 4.3 below.

Knowledge management

Knowledge management can enable sports organizations to act more intelligently about opportunities. In the past, there was an emphasis on quantifiable outputs such as total quality management and business process engineering but this has changed with the emphasis on learning organizations. As Charband and Jafari Navimipour (2018:1456) state "since resources of knowledge are important, human energy and time have been invested in knowledge management to increase the value of knowledge." This has meant that knowledge is being used to understand a sports organization's core competences, which facilitates market progress. The increased digitalization of the sports industry has meant knowledge is important to an organization's strategic focus. Sports organizations have their own methods

TABLE 4.3 Social entrepreneurship transfer effectiveness criteria

Criteria	Main advantage and disadvantage
Economic development	Advantage – Financial impact of the social venture.
	Disadvantage – Assumption of monetary gain.
Human capital	Advantage – Focuses on developing individuals that can transfer knowledge about social entrepreneurship.
	Disadvantage – If employees leave they take the knowledge with them.
Market impact	Advantage – Focuses on the performance and likely future developments.
	Disadvantage – Can take time before people know about social entrepreneurship.
Opportunity costs	Advantage – Considers alternative approaches to social entrepreneurship.
	Disadvantage – Hard to ascertain what the risks are in terms of social entrepreneurship.
Political	Advantage – There are many political considerations in sport.
	Disadvantage – Political connections required to ensure the success of sport social entrepreneurship.
Public value	Advantage – Addresses the need for sport services in the community.
	Disadvantage – Over-reliance on funding for sport social entrepreneurship.
Scientific capital	Advantage – Easier for commercial sport ventures to use intellectual capital.
	Disadvantage – Hard to measure the impact of sport social enterprises.

for acquiring knowledge for social entrepreneurship. Sport managers have several techniques for assimilating knowledge including through their absorptive capacity. This means absorbing knowledge in a way that makes a difference to their organization. Sport managers can benefit from understanding how to acquire the knowledge that enhances their competitiveness. Absorptive capacity involves accessing the potential of knowledge via an acquisition and assimilation process then realizing its potential in terms of transformation (Hoarau, 2014).

Knowledge is defined as "the use of skills and experience to add intelligence to information to make decisions or provide reliable ground for action" (Hoarau, 2014). To develop ideas about social ventures, knowledge is needed to enable a sports organization to identify social causes then plan a course of action. The existing knowledge pool of an organization needs to be renewed by adding external sources of knowledge. Hoarau (2014) suggests there are three ways to understand the role of knowledge in innovation processes: residing in individuals, as a transferable commodity and through participation. Knowledge is stored by individuals and can be transmitted to others. This involves a mental process of appropriating knowledge for specific uses. After the knowledge has been identified by individuals, it can then be transmitted through communication. This helps pass information on to others about the usefulness of the knowledge. Society uses knowledge as a way to introduce ideas and bring about change.

Knowledge spillover-based strategic entrepreneurship is defined as "unintentional knowledge flows that can be used for strategic purposes to network entities other than the creators for innovative, risk taking, proactive and competitive business reasons" (Ferreira et al., 2017:162). Being a social entrepreneur involves undertaking entrepreneurial actions that include a non-profit component. Social entrepreneurship can be beneficial for the creator but also for the recipients if the venture is used in the right way. The knowledge spillover theory of entrepreneurship suggests "entrepreneurial opportunities consist of a set of ideas endogenously created by investments in new knowledge that enable the creation of future products absent on the market" (Caiazza et al., 2019:2). This is important in sport entrepreneurial ecosystems as knowledge from other sources can be applied in business ventures.

Tacit knowledge refers to knowledge an individual has by virtue of experience. This form of knowledge once transferred in a written way becomes explicit. Due to the personal way tacit knowledge is accumulated it can be hard to share. This is because knowledge in a holistic sense is hard to describe and relies on the interpretation of the listener (Scuotto et al., 2017). To further elucidate tacit knowledge it is helpful to understand its cognitive and technical dimensions (Nonaka, 1991). The cognitive dimensions refer to the beliefs and values manifested in the way information is perceived by an individual. This involves assessing the ideas based on their relevance and usefulness. Some of the information imparted as part of the knowledge collection process will be more valuable than others. Thus, assessing what information is known and readily available compared to what is needed is required. The technical dimension refers to know-how as it relies on more scientific assessments of its relevance. Some of this technical information is acquired easily but other forms require a more individualized approach. This means the context in which the knowledge is imparted needs to be analyzed.

Knowledge can be tacit or explicit depending on its role in the environment. Tacit knowledge normally takes the form of localized processes or practices that are hard to codify (Hoarau, 2014). This means tacit knowledge is embedded in an environment and shared through direct interaction. Explicit knowledge is easier to transfer as it involves information that can be explained more easily. Both tacit and explicit forms of knowledge contribute to the building of social networks. To enable knowledge to be interpreted it requires a shared social and mental space (Sundbo, 1998). For new knowledge to be created it needs to be acquired but also translated into accessible knowledge. This occurs via accumulated social interactions (Nonaka and Takeuchi, 1995). As knowledge is a product of an individual's know-how and experiences, it helps when there is trust amongst social network members. Knowledge brokers can do this by overcoming barriers of having knowledge that is hard to share. Broadly defined, knowledge brokers are individuals who "support innovation by connecting, recombining and transferring to new contexts otherwise disconnected pools of ideas" (Hoarau, 2014:139). Entrepreneurial ecosystems involve knowledge brokers who exchange or share knowledge amongst various entities including businesses, government and citizens.

A key lubricator of knowledge spillovers is social networks, which facilitate the sharing of information. Knowledge accumulated from social networks tends to be transferred more easily when there are high levels of interdependence amongst network members. The amount of knowledge flowing in and out matters for entrepreneurial ecosystems. In addition, the quality of knowledge converted depends on the knowledge-creating capabilities of firms in an ecosystem. Knowledge is circulated in networks via organizational- or individual-based links. In sport communities, both organizations and individuals work on mutually recognizable issues. They recognize that the success of the sports industry is the result of collective knowledge-building activities. There is more knowledge connectivity in society because of the ability of firms and individuals to transfer knowledge through their social networks. The amount and type of knowledge exchanged will depend on the reciprocity of network members.

Market knowledge competence is defined as "the processes that generate and integrate market knowledge" (Ozkaya et al., 2015:310). Organizations need to develop their market knowledge as a competitive asset that helps increase their performance. Once they have developed a competence in obtaining market knowledge it can help them deliver strategic outcomes. There are three main components of market knowledge competence: customer knowledge competence, competitor knowledge competence and marketing-research and development. It is important to find out what needs customers have for new products and services. This can involve focusing on what products or services competitors are investing in and the amount spent on innovation.

Brooker and Joppe (2014:500) define innovation as "introducing novel concepts that are potentially valuable to both new and existing customers that differentiate an organization." This business perspective of innovation needs to be modified to other contexts depending on its usage. Market-based innovation is defined as "innovations that depart from serving existing mainstream markets and that create a set of fringe and usually new customer values for emerging markets" (Ozkaya et al., 2015:311). Increasingly sports organizations are using market-based innovations as a way to target potentially lucrative new markets that have not been considered before. As technology develops it is important to focus on advances that might lead to the development of new products or service markets. This includes designing products for specific customer groups that are different to the current customers. This occurred with female sportswear being introduced into the market as a distinct market segment. In the past many sports clothing companies focused more on the male market but this has changed with the rise in interest by females in certain sports. Adding a new line of clothing specifically for females has resulted in increased sales growth and profits. In order to assess properly the information received there needs to be the appropriate knowledge-management techniques that involve practice, culture, commitment and training. These are stated in Table 4.4 below.

Reputation management

Sports organizations have typically been viewed as providers of entertainment services but less as knowledge providers. This has changed with the use of mobile technology and social media in sport. To benefit from the fourth industrial revolution in terms of increased usage of artificial intelligence, sports organizations need to transform themselves into knowledge providers. This means emphasizing their service ecosystem and the multiple networks that concurrently interact to produce innovation by protecting their reputation.

Reputation management involves practices used to cope with changing interpretations and expectations (Hogarth et al., 2018). More organizations are focusing on managing their reputation due to environmental pressures and competition. Reputations evolve over time depending on situations so it is important for organizations to keep a favorable position in the marketplace. To do this they must consider all stakeholders involved with the organization and assess potential risk. There are different factors affecting reputation including governance mechanisms, workplace culture, regulatory procedures and financial performance (Christensen and Raynor, 2003). Each of these factors is important to organizations wanting to maintain their reputation in the long term.

Organizational leaders need to focus on how to be socially responsible and deliver on promises. This means communicating to stakeholders in a timely manner about potential risks and how they will be managed. The reputation of an organization is tied to how stakeholders perceive them and the way they handle crises. Organizations need to show that they care about what they are doing and their impact on others. This means including social initiatives as a way to improve their reputation. Traditional funding in sport is waning, meaning new revenue sources are needed. Some sports organizations receive only a fraction of the government support they did in the past and need to find additional funding options. Sports organizations need to think strategically about opening the way for more social entrepreneurship. This will enable a deeper engagement between sports organizations and their community, which can provide the impetus for social change.

Conclusion

Most studies on social entrepreneurship take a single level analysis based on the perceptions of one organization. This means the sport environmental ecosystem context in which they evolve is overlooked. The presence of different kinds of relationships in sport means that a multilevel approach better represents what is happening in the environment. I posit that adopting a multilevel vision of social entrepreneurship can enhance the functioning of sports organizations. Based on my analysis, I have observed that most sport managers tend to focus on philanthropy and underestimate the power of social entrepreneurship and entrepreneurial ecosystems. This lack of attention means the attitude to social entrepreneurship by sport managers needs to change. By taking a multilevel view, sport managers can

TABLE 4.4 Knowledge management in sport social enterprises

Type	Examples
Knowledge management practices	Formal
	– Attend seminars and training events about sport developments.
	– Read new articles and books about sport research.
	– Collaborate with other sports organizations to collect information.
	Informal
	– Discuss with other individuals about sport developments.
	– Chat about new sport practices that are affecting the industry.
	– Ask acquaintances and colleagues about their opinions.
Knowledge culture	– Discuss new ideas and ways they can change sport.
	– Improvement is part of the organizational culture.
	– Problem-solving is encouraged.
	– Responsibility is taken to learn about new innovations.
Commitment	– Learning new things is valued.
	– Individuals have a role in disseminating information about sport.
	– Rewards are a way we can encourage sport social enterprise.
	– Extra effort is taken to apply knowledge to a sports context.
	– Continual improvement is important.
Training	– Learning is important in facilitating social entrepreneurship.
	– Knowledge learnt through education programs is applied to sport.
	– Experiences are shared about sport practices.

maximize the interactions between different types of stakeholders. This will enable a more systematic approach to social entrepreneurship to develop and allow sport managers to better manage social agreements.

As sports organizations tend to belong to an alliance network we need to understand the competitive mechanisms that exist. This involves extending the current boundaries to incorporate alliance, networks and other collaborative agreements (Arco-Castro et al., 2018). The different levels of activity that sports organizations are engaged in need to be analyzed more carefully. In other words, asserting that sports organizations act alone is incorrect due to the plethora of existing network relationships. The boundary of the sports organization has broadened due to overlapping interests in many entities. Coopetition is more common amongst sports organizations and affects decisions on whether or not to conduct social entrepreneurship. Extending the boundary of the sports organization to the intra- and inter-organizational level can better reflect the state of social entrepreneurial ventures. This will enable a better typology of social entrepreneurship in sport to emerge.

References

Acs, Z. J., Autio, E. and Szerb, L. (2014) "National systems of entrepreneurship: Measurement issues and policy implications," *Research Policy*, 43(3): 476–494.

Adomako, S., Danso, A., Boso, N. and Narteh, B. (2018) "Entrepreneurial alertness and new venture performance: Facilitating roles of networking capability," *International Small Business Journal*, 36(5): 453–472.

Arco-Castro, L., Lopez-Perez, M., Perez-Lopez, M. and Rodriguez-Ariza, L. (2018) "Corporate philanthropy and employee engagement," *Review of Managerial Science*, in press.

Audretsch, D. B. and Belitski, M. (2017) "Entrepreneurial ecosystems in cities: Establishing the framework conditions," *The Journal of Technology Transfer*, 42(5): 1030–1051.

Ayuso, S., Ángel Rodríguez, M. and Enric Ricart, J. (2006) "Using stakeholder dialogue as a source for new ideas: A dynamic capability underlying sustainable innovation," *Corporate Governance: The International Journal of Business in Society*, 6(4): 475–490.

Boies, K., Fiset, J. and Gill, H. (2015) "Communication and trust are key: Unlocking the relationship between leadership and team performance and creativity," *The Leadership Quarterly*, 26(6): 1080–1094.

Brooker, E. and Joppe, M. (2014) "Developing a tourism innovation typology: Leveraging liminal insights," *Journal of Travel Research*, 53(4): 500–508.

Bui, H., Kuan, A. and Chu, T. (2018) "Female entrepreneurship in patriarchal society: Motivation and challenges," *Journal of Small Business & Entrepreneurship*, 30(4): 325–343.

Caiazza, R., Belitski, M. and Audretsch, D. (2019) "From latent to emergent entrepreneurship: The knowledge spillover construction role," *The Journal of Technology Transfer*, in press, 1–11.

Charband, Y. and Jafari Navimipour, N. (2018) "Knowledge sharing mechanisms in the education: A systematic review of the state of the art literature and recommendations for future research," *Kybernetes*, 47(7): 1456–1490.

Christensen, C. and Raynor, M. (2003) *The innovators solution: Creating and sustaining successful growth*. Cambridge, MA: Harvard Business School Press.

Cohen, B. (2006) "Sustainable valley entrepreneurial ecosystems," *Business Strategy and the Environment*, 15(1): 1–14.

Estevao, C., Cruz, R., Ferreira, J. and Ratten, V. (2017) "Contemporary approaches to performance evaluation of international hotel groups in Portugal," *Journal for Global Business Advancement*, 11(2): 173–192.

Ferreira, J. J., Ratten, V. and Dana, L. P. (2017) "Knowledge spillover-based strategic entrepreneurship," *International Entrepreneurship and Management Journal*, 13(1): 161–167.

Figueiredo, V. and Franco, M. (2018) "Factors influencing cooperator satisfaction: A study applied to wine cooperatives in Portugal," *Journal of Cleaner Production*, 191, 15–25.

Freeman, R. E. 1984. *Strategic management: A stakeholder approach*. Boston, MA: Pitman Publishing.

Grönroos, C. and Voima, P. (2013) "Critical service logic: Making sense of value creation and co-creation," *Journal of the Academy of Marketing Science*, 41(2): 133–150.

Hjalager, A. M. (2002) "Repairing innovation defectiveness in tourism," *Tourism Management*, 23(5): 465–474.

Hoarau, H. (2014) "Knowledge acquisition and assimilation in tourism-innovation processes," *Scandinavian Journal of Hospitality and Tourism*, 14(2): 135–151.

Hogarth, K., Hutchinson, M. and Scaife, W. (2018) "Corporate philanthropy, reputation risk management and shareholder value: A study of Australian corporate giving," *Journal of Business Ethics*, 151: 375–390.

Isenberg, D. J. (2010) "How to start an entrepreneurial revolution," *Harvard Business Review*, 88(6): 41–50.

Kirzner, I. M. (1979) *Perception, opportunity, and profit: Studies in the theory of entrepreneurship.* Chicago, IL: University of Chicago Press.

Light, I. and Dana, L. P. (2013) "Boundaries of social capital in entrepreneurship," *Entrepreneurship Theory and Practice*, 37(3): 603–624.

Lusch, R. F. and Vargo, S. L. (2014) *The service-dominant logic of marketing: Dialog, debate, and directions.* London: Routledge.

Malecki, E. J. (2018) "Entrepreneurship and entrepreneurial ecosystems," *Geography Compass*, 12(3): e12359.

Mayer, R., Davis, J. and Schoorman, F. (1995) "An integrative model of organizational trust," *Academy of Management Review*, 20(3): 709–734.

Mazzei, M. (2018) "Strategic entrepreneurship: Content, process, context and outcomes," *International Entrepreneurship and Management Journal*, 14(3): 657–670.

Miles, M. P. and Morrison, M. (2018) "An effectual leadership perspective for developing rural entrepreneurial ecosystems," *Small Business Economics*, 1–17.

Neumeyer, X. and Corbett, A. C. (eds) (2017) "Entrepreneurial ecosystems: Weak metaphor or genuine concept?" In *The great debates in entrepreneurship* (pp. 35–45). London: Emerald Publishing Limited.

Neumeyer, X., Santos, S. C., Caetano, A. and Kalbfleisch, P. (2018) "Entrepreneurship ecosystems and women entrepreneurs: A social capital and network approach," *Small Business Economics*, in press, 1–15.

Nonaka, I. (1991) "The knowledge creating company," *Harvard Business Review*, November–December: 96–104.

Nonaka, I. and Takeuchi, H. (1995) *The knowledge-creating company: How Japanese companies create the dynamics of innovation.* Oxford: Oxford University Press.

Ozkaya, H. E., Droge, C., Hult, G. T. M., Calantone, R. and Ozkaya, E. (2015) "Market orientation, knowledge competence, and innovation," *International Journal of Research in Marketing*, 32(3): 309–318.

Pfeffer, J. and Salancik, G. (1978) *The external control of organizations: A resource dependence perspective.* New York: Harper & Row.

Poldner, K., Shrivastava, P. and Branzei, O. (2017) "Embodied multi-discursivity: An aesthetic process approach to sustainable entrepreneurship," *Business & Society*, 56(2): 214–252.

Quarter, J., Sousa, J., Richmond, B. J. and Carmichael, I. (2001) "Comparing member-based organizations within a social economy framework," *Nonprofit and voluntary sector quarterly*, 30(2): 351–375.

Ratten, V. (2004) "Learning and information dissemination in logistics alliances," *Asia Pacific Journal of Marketing and Logistics*, 16(4): 65–81.

Ratten, V. (2010) "Developing a theory of sport-based entrepreneurship," *Journal of Management & Organization*, 16(4): 557–565.

Ratten, V. (2017) "Eco-innovation and competitiveness in the Barossa Valley wine region," *Competitiveness Review*, 28(3): 318–331.

Ratten, V. and Tajeddini, K. (2018) "Women's entrepreneurship and internationalization: Patterns and trends," *International Journal of Sociology and Social Policy*, 38(9/10): 780–793.

Roundy, P. T., Bradshaw, M. and Brockman, B. K. (2018) "The emergence of entrepreneurial ecosystems: A complex adaptive systems approach," *Journal of Business Research*, 86, 1–10.

Scuotto, V., Del Giudice, M., Bresciani, S. and Meissner, D. (2017) "Knowledge-driven preferences in informal inbound open innovation modes: An explorative view on small to medium enterprises," *Journal of Knowledge Management*, 21(3): 640–655.

Sorensen, F. (2007) "The geographies of social networks and innovation in tourism," *Tourism Geographies*, 9(1): 22–48.

Spilling, O. R. (1996) "The entrepreneurial system: On entrepreneurship in the context of a mega-event," *Journal of Business Research*, 36(1): 91–103.

Stangler, D. and Bell-Masterson, J. (2015) "Measuring an entrepreneurial ecosystem," in *Kauffman Foundation Research Series on City, Metro, and Regional Entrepreneurship*, online, 16.

Stock, M., Zacharias, N. A. and Schnellbaecher, A. (2017) "How do strategy and leadership styles jointly affect co-development and its innovation outcomes?" *Journal of Product Innovation Management*, 34(2): 201–222.

Suddaby, R. (2010) "Construct clarity in theories of management and organization," *Academy of Management Review*, 35(1): 346–357.

Sundbo, J. (1998) *The theory of innovation: Enterpreneurs, technology and strategy.* Cheltenham: Edward Elgar Publishing.

Tang, J., Kacmar, K. M. M. and Busenitz, L. (2012) "Entrepreneurial alertness in the pursuit of new opportunities," *Journal of Business Venturing*, 27(1): 77–94.

Tushman, M. L. (1977) "Special boundary roles in the innovation process," *Administrative Science Quarterly*, 22(4): 587–605.

Welty Peachey, J., Musser, A., Shin, N. and Cohen, A. (2018) "Interrogating the motivations of sport for development and peace practitioners," *International Review for the Sociology of Sport*, 53(7): 767–787.

Yang, X. and Andersson, D. (2018) "Spatial aspects of entrepreneurship and innovation," *The Annals of Regional Science*, 61: 457–462.

Zhou, R. and Kaplanidou, K. (2018) "Building social capital from sport event participation: An exploration of the social impacts of participating events on the community," *Sport Management Review*, 21: 491–503.

5

STRATEGIES FOR SOCIAL ENTREPRENEURSHIP

Integrating social entrepreneurship into sport

Sport entrepreneurs need to be assertive in order to venture into new businesses and try out new ideas. Due to the need to be visionary the personal traits associated with entrepreneurship include innovation, initiative, action and competition. Fortunato (2014:389) defines an entrepreneur as

> an individual (or part of a group of individuals) who has created a new business venture within a place to offer a new product or service, bundle of products or services, or price/value relationship that adds value to markets within that community.

Thus, adding value is an important component of sport entrepreneurship, particularly when it is related to social business ventures. This emphasis on value creation can be traced back to the origins of the word entrepreneur. The word "entrepreneur" means someone who has the ability to combine ideas and resources. This means, in a broad sense, entrepreneurs have the capability to bring together resources in order to create value in society.

Throughout the sport sector, individuals and organizations are discussing the need for social entrepreneurship to address pressing issues. Social enterprises play a role in reforming the marketplace by providing a collective response to societal problems. Social entrepreneurship is needed in sport as a way to combat the negative perceptions of cheating in sport. There are five social criteria used to analyze social enterprises: (1) community aim, (2) group initiative, (3) collective decision-making, (4) participatory nature and (5) limited profit distribution (Rinkinen et al., 2016). The sport community plays an important role in facilitating the growth and development of social enterprises. Particularly in rural communities, sport plays a central role in social cohesion and interaction amongst members of the community. The group initiative involves how well sport entities come together for a common purpose. In order to build social enterprises it is important that groups share a common vision. Collective decision-making refers to a number of people reaching the same consensus about the benefits of social entrepreneurship (Ferreira et al., 2017). This is important in order to gain support from multiple stakeholders. The participatory nature of social entrepreneurship involves different people having a say in the direction that the sport social enterprise takes. This helps to build an entrepreneurial spirit in the sport community. Limited profit distribution means that whilst financial outcomes are a goal of the social enterprise the level of the profits is not as important as the social outcome.

There has been a steady increase in the amount of scholarly enquiry into social entrepreneurship but less centered on the sports industry. The ability to act upon an opportunity that incorporates a social mission is important for the success of sports organizations and needs to be further integrated into scholarship. Given that sports organizations are already involved in entrepreneurship, it is useful to see how social forms can create new ideas. Social entrepreneurship is a factor that determines how a sports organization implements profit and social objectives. Sports organizations use social entrepreneurship through adopting and adapting already existing innovations. This results in the pace of social entrepreneurship in sport being determined mainly by the speed at which social causes can be linked to financial outcomes.

The process of integrating social entrepreneurship into a sports organization follows a number of stages. First, there needs to be an awareness and understanding about the role of social entrepreneurship in sport. This involves having a responsible attitude to social problems and acknowledging the role sports organizations play in this regard. Formal structures need to be set up in order to establish social entrepreneurship business models. Next, there needs to be a commitment to social entrepreneurship by providing resources and time. This legitimizes the practice of social entrepreneurship and helps drive momentum around social issues. Once this process has been accepted there needs to be an action plan to integrate social entrepreneurship into management strategies. This will help make transparent what is needed to be done by the sports organization in order to facilitate social entrepreneurship. Once the sports organization has started to be more entrepreneurial then its performance can be assessed. This will enable the philosophical underpinnings of the organization to incorporate more social objectives.

This chapter enhances social entrepreneurship theory by extending it to a sport context. The chapter corroborates prior research on social entrepreneurship by elucidating the moderating role of social responsibility. This includes focusing on the role of non-profits and volunteer management in the success of social enterprises.

Social responsibility, philanthropy and charity

The concept of social responsibility, philanthropy and charity in sport needs to be re-shaped into social entrepreneurship. In sport there has been more of a focus on non-profit or social issues than linking it to business purposes. Social entrepreneurship enables the combination of non-profit and profit initiatives, which can help sports organizations act in a more professional manner whilst maintaining their social mission. Social entrepreneurship allows the creation of business ventures that can generate monetary gain whilst progressing social equity. Sport has been criticized in some instances for being too focused on commercial endeavors so incorporating social missions can enable reputational benefits. I believe that sport should be used more as a context for social entrepreneurship. Specifically, I suggest expanding our understanding of social entrepreneurship to better reflect its meaning in sport. There can be a discrepancy between how sports organizations define social entrepreneurship and how it is practiced. They tend not to define it in the same way that academics do but rather relate it to social responsibility and social management issues.

The theory of legitimacy has been used to understand corporate philanthropy and social responsibility. Arco-Castro et al. (2018:3) define the theory of legitimacy as "a generalized perception or assumption that the actions of an entity are desirable, proper or appropriate within a socially-constructed system of norms, values, beliefs and definitions." This definition implies that there is an understanding amongst entities in a community about ways of behaving. This forms a social contract and impacts the relationships between organizations in their market environment. Sports organizations that are committed to maintaining their reputation need to comply with the social contract in order to be perceived as being committed to their stakeholders. This will enhance existing relationships and help forge new ones.

Non-profit organizations are characterized by their diversity and include "religious congregations, universities, hospitals, museums, homeless shelters, civil rights groups, labor unions, political parties and environmental organisations" (Boris and Steuerle, 2006:66). This heterogeneity amongst non-profits means there is a range of ways they are defined in the literature. Common to most definitions of non-profits is how there are not positive financial benefits as the revenue either gets reinvested or expended. Normally most non-profits have both paid staff and volunteers although the emphasis is normally on the unpaid workforce. The key objective of a non-profit is usually socially motivated and affects its clients and customers. The focus of most non-profits tends to be around advocacy and mutual benefit activity that provides assistance to those in need. There is a range of services that non-profits provide to the community and this includes education, health and social services. In addition, the creative industry tends to rely on non-profits due to their emphasis on creativity rather than financial gain. This means the arts and cultural sectors have a number of non-profits that rely both on government grants and private donations.

As more government services have been privatized there has been a need to provide additional social services (Peterson, 2018). This has affected the way non-profit providers interact in the market and has influenced some to become social enterprises. In addition, the advent of businesses incorporating a social mission in their products or services has increased (Ratten, 2019). This has led to more consumers questioning the social role they play in the buying experience (Zietlow, 2001). Non-profit providers are acting more business-like as a way to attract more interest. There is also a blurring between profit and non-profit providers in terms of how they market themselves. Competition has intensified in the market but has also created new challenges (Ferreira and Ratten, 2018). In conjunction with the emphasis on social responsibility has been the increased interest in social problem-solving practices. This includes different interpretations of the role non-profits play in society and has changed them from relying on grants or fundraising to focusing on creating earned social ventures (Will et al., 2018). This has advanced the practice of non-profits but has also made them introduce new ideas such as social return on investment into the market.

Financially empowered non-profits have eight main characteristics (Brinckerhoff, 1995). First, their revenue exceeds their expenses which makes them long-term sustainable business ventures. Second, they have a cash operating reserve, which means they can independently pay for services rendered. This distinguishes them from non-profits who are reliant on funding for everyday expenses (Morris et al., 2018). Third, some of their income comes from endowment earnings. For large non-profits, particularly universities, these endowment funds have become an important source of finance. Fourth, there is information-sharing about budgeting and finance that helps ensure future plans are fulfilled. This includes knowledge about financial procedures that ensure multiple entities know about the financial conditions. Fifth, there is an emphasis on social missions in terms of responding to community needs. This involves having ethical procedures in place to ensure support is given when needed. Sixth, debt financing is used as a way of building initiatives that might take some initial financial resources to start. Seventh, non-traditional sources of income are generated that lessen the need to rely on other funding mechanisms. These finance options ensure elasticity with resource requirements. Eighth, there is flexibility in finances, which means resources can be redeployed when needed. This is useful in times of economic distress when money is needed for certain causes.

Self-determination theory is a way of understanding the motivations for pursuing social interests in sport (Welty Peachey et al., 2018). This theory suggests individuals are motivated for extrinsic or intrinsic reasons. Extrinsic reasons refer to behavior based on rewards such as money, pressure or title. Intrinsic reasons relate to more individual-based behaviors such as enjoyment or a sense of well-being. Both types of reasons can exist on a continuum that relates to the level of intensity for each type of behavior. Ryan and Deci (2000) suggest that there is also another category of motivation, referred to as amotivation, which involves a lack of interest or reason for action. This means individuals may have no inclination to behave in a certain way because they perceive no positive or negative effects. In addition, within extrinsic motivation there are four main types: external regulation, introjected regulation, identified regulation and integrated regulation (Ryan and Deci, 2000). External regulation means outside sport bodies influence the actions of individuals whilst introjected regulation refers to a need to oversee the playing of sport. Identified regulation often occurs when new medical or technology advances change the nature of sport. This relates to integrated regulation, which occurs when sport takes into account societal changes such as new rules or policies.

Non-governmental organizations (NGOs) have been referred to as civil society or third sector organizations. Broadly defined, they relate to an organization not in the private or public sector but, rather, focused on social endeavors. They are reliant on charity for their functioning and use volunteers for many daily functions. Their non-profit status has meant they are not focused solely on profits or perform-ance but rather on social missions. This enables them to have more autonomy and independence than other types of organizations. By design they are self-governing but are dependent on funding that is linked to the popularity of different social issues in society. They serve an important role in the global economy by helping disadvantaged members and provide services in areas that are neglected. This helps fill a gap that exists between the services provided by the private sector and those offered by the government.

The three main functions of NGOs are service delivery, educational provision and public policy advocacy (Stromquist, 1998). Service delivery means offering relief through providing services not offered by other entities and can include wel-fare, housing and food. Educational provision means teaching skills such as literacy and language to underprivileged segments of society. In order to foster community cohesion and increase living standards, it is important that education is provided. Public policy advocacy relates to minority government initiatives in a region and where possible helping people to obtain better services.

Despite the known benefits of social entrepreneurship, there are few studies in the sport management literature but this will change as more researchers become interested in this topic (Ratten and Tajeddini, 2019). There are different reasons why social entrepreneurship is important in sport and these include value orien-tation, community involvement and extrinsic rewards. For those involved with the sports industry many are volunteers who have a love of sport. This means they will be attracted to any business venture related to sport. Thus, it can be easier to get volunteer involvement in sport ventures, especially those with a social mission. Kim et al. (2018:375) state that volunteers are "a highly diverse group and frequently represent different nationalities and cultures, gender, age, career backgrounds, personal characteristics and previous volunteer experiences." As social entrepreneur-ship has a non-profit component, it can provide a way for individuals to connect both with their love of sport and the ability to help others. This enables them to gain a new perspective about the role of sport in society by doing something they consider worthwhile. It can help individuals to be perceived as more caring and make use of their interests for a good cause. Part of this involvement means indi-viduals expressing their pride in sport but also being proud of the way sport can be integrated into social ventures. Social entrepreneurship involves interacting with others so that people who love sport can develop their interpersonal contacts. In addition, there are rewards from social ventures including interacting with others who are also interested in sport.

Volunteering is a large part of the sports industry and has contributed to the link between sport and the community. Sport events bring benefits to a community including increased attachment and civic pride. The social interactions occurring at sport events help build social capital amongst participants and a sense of camaraderie. This solidifies sport events as being crucial for the social cohesion of a community but also in terms of creating a sense of belonging. This enables people from different ethnic and religious beliefs to come together to share a sense of achievement from associating with a sport team; it helps create bonds amongst individuals and transcends social boundaries.

Volunteers are motivated by normative, affective and utilitarian incentives. Normative incentives involve a sense of purpose about what they are achieving in terms of how they can help others. This desire is embedded in having a genuine concern for others and how they can contribute to solving problems. Affective incentives involve having a sense of solidarity with others. This incorporates the social cohesion that comes from being a volunteer. Utilitarian incentives involve the associated benefits derived from interacting with others for a social purpose. This includes having a better understanding about the needs of others.

Social ventures

In social entrepreneurship research, there are different types of industry that are more conducive to social ventures. Industries that have a high percentage of non-profit entities such as sport are likely to be more involved in social transactions. Social enterprises can be classified in a number of different ways including function, size, temperament, goals, priorities, customer mix, growth rate, technological orientation and internationalization pattern (Mota et al., 2019). Function refers to the main purpose of the social enterprise in terms of what it does and the role it plays in the economy. Some social enterprises act as marketing mechanisms for a particular cause whilst others are focused on specific issues such as poverty alleviation. The size of social enterprises differs from very small or micro managed businesses that employ one or two people to medium- and large-sized enterprises. Size is a relative concept as in some countries large enterprises refer to more than 1000 employees whilst in other countries it means over 100 employees. In addition, size might not be a factor in the popularity of a social enterprise due to word of mouth and other low-cost forms of advertising. Some social enterprises take time to develop so they might start small but then partner with other organizations to help share their efforts. This involves structuring activities in a way that facilitates collaboration.

Social enterprises can be online, rather than physical entities, so it can be easier to share information through digital means. Online social enterprises have the advantage of having an online platform that can be replicated in other countries. There can be a central authority structure that plans the international activities for all their social enterprises. The temperament of social enterprises differs depending on the level of passion engaged by individuals. Some social enterprises might be very proactive about solving a social problem and this is related to the intensity of their efforts. Social enterprises that touch on a sensitive subject might have more emotional attachment than others. This is then reflected in the dedication of members towards a social cause. Temperament can be measured in a number of different ways including risk-taking activities that will influence the reputation of the social enterprise in the market. Whilst some social enterprises take a slow and careful approach to growth, others are determined to grow quickly. The goals a social enterprise has will be related to the way they have developed their business interests. Some goals are purely altruistic whilst other goals might be tied to the interests of certain individuals. This makes leadership an important facet of any social enterprise as leaders can steer the social enterprise towards achieving certain goals. Leaders who are considered transformational focus on major changes that their social enterprise can make to society. Depending on the focus of the social enterprise this can include numerous programs related to sport such as recycling initiatives or the use of sustainable materials. Social enterprises have different priorities that affect their management practices. In craft or artisan types of social enterprises the priority might be in retaining craft skills that can be passed down through generations. Increasingly there has been an interest in artisan entrepreneurship and this can relate to ensuring the longevity of traditional sports, such as archery, which might not be as popular anymore but has a cultural significance. Other priorities for social enterprises might be in the way they configure their enterprise in terms of process and strategy.

The decision-making style of a social enterprise will be influenced by a manager's attitude towards change. Some managers will prefer a more growth-orientated strategy that is reflected in the launch of new goods. For other managers, a more wait-and-see approach will appeal as they transition into higher growth categories. Depending on how their products are perceived by customers there will be a process of experimentation. This is reflected in the competitiveness of the sports industry and the types of products championed by social entrepreneurs. The ability of social entrepreneurs to grow will depend on the level and type of help they receive from others. As the sports industry has a high proportion of amateur clubs and volunteers compared to other industries, it might be more attuned to the need for social entrepreneurship. This is due to there being a strong community sentiment about the role sport plays in society.

Sport-based social enterprises can be analyzed according to their time horizon for growth. Social enterprises that are run on a need basis normally only have a short-term focus that is reflected in having a low entrepreneurial orientation. This means managers of these social enterprises have a more reactive approach to market fluctuations. The level of technology investment is normally low and the financing is risk averse. This allows the social enterprise to be shut down and relocated to other areas more quickly. Being able to move in this way means the economic motives are focused on a break-even perspective rather than purely profits. The reward for these survival types of social enterprises is in contributing to alleviating some social problems through sport-related social enterprises.

Lifestyle-based social entrepreneurship

Lifestyle-based social enterprises are set up because individuals are interested in living a certain way and this is reflected in business practices. Some entrepreneurs like certain sports due to the way they can interact with their lifestyle. This is evident in the increasing popularity of nature-based sports such as surfing. Along with this trend has been the interest in social enterprises related to sport. The environment such as having clean water and protected nature reserves are important social issues that can be reflected in the mission of a social enterprise. Normally lifestyle social enterprises are developed by a group of people involved in a sport. The structure of lifestyle social enterprises is simple and reflected in income substitution for a certain way of life. Social enterprises who have a more managed or aggressive growth strategy are likely to be more involved in strategically thinking about long-term plans. This involves leveraging existing projects to build bigger ones. Taking a wealth creating approach to the social enterprise means the entrepreneurial orientation is higher. This can involve the use of more formalized financial partners such as banks and private investors.

Sport managers differ from entrepreneurs as they are involved with organizing activities instead of proactively seeking new opportunities. Whilst a certain degree of organization skills is still needed by entrepreneurs, more important is foreseeing potential gaps in the market. There is a positive link between social entrepreneurship and psychological empowerment, which highlights the importance of including activities with an intrinsic value in business practices. Sport is part of our culture and transcends social barriers. The goal for most people participating in sport is to improve their physical fitness but other factors such as improved mental well-being can occur. This means that whilst most sports have some kind of physical activity there can also be benefits from increased levels of social engagement. People playing sport exert energy levels above their normal levels that produce a psychological effect.

Entrepreneurship and small business is context dependent, which affects the success of business ventures. Increasingly there has been interest in culture as a way of understanding how language, symbols and behavior affect entrepreneurship. Due to the variety of cultural contexts in the international business environment, it becomes important to focus on the way culture affects entrepreneurial intention. This can occur at the individual, business, community or regional level depending on the situation. Lifestyle reasons for entrepreneurship are also a way of understanding cultural conditions in society. For some, work/life balance is important and this determines the kind of business ventures they are involved in. The connection to the environment is crucial for others with eco-entrepreneurship and social entrepreneurship being popular. There is more lifestyle mobility in communities due to individuals' ongoing semi-permanent moves. In the past, there was reluctance in people to move often and if they did it tended to be for migration reasons. This has changed with individuals being required to move for lifestyle or work reasons and has led to a trend towards more lifestyle entrepreneurs who pursue businesses for lifestyle reasons that have a financial objective.

Diversity and social entrepreneurship policy

Diversity management is defined as "the specific programmes, policies and practices that organizations have developed and implemented to manage a diverse workforce effectively and to promote organizational equality" (Dennissen et al., 2018:2). Sports organizations tend to implement similar practices regarding social entrepreneurship without much context specificity. The effects of social entrepreneurship are understood to be the same for all sports organizations despite some having greater effect than others. There needs to be social entrepreneurship training as one policy will not fit with all sports organizations. Rather there are different social entrepreneurship policies that can fall within the professional or amateur sport category. In addition, there is an intersectionality between amateur and professional sport that needs to be considered with social entrepreneurship. Professional sports organizations have affiliations with smaller amateur associations that are often the drivers of social entrepreneurship policies.

Sport policy provides a useful way of including social objectives through business ventures. In addition, sport policy can include goals related to public policy such as sustainability concerns. Dyllick and Hockerts (2002:130) state that sustainability "embodies the promise of societal evolution towards a more equitable and wealthy world in which the natural environment and our cultural achievements are preserved for generations to come." Due to the existence of a vast number of sport playing fields there are environmental facts that need to be taken into account. This stems from the increased interest in sustainability initiatives such as recycling that can influence sport practices. Sustainable entrepreneurs provide a bridge between ideas, resources and nature. Thus, sustainable entrepreneurs in sport combine social and economic factors including financing and funding with regard to sport issues. Some general community concerns can be integrated into sport policy. This is evident in the building of new sport stadiums that benefit sport teams but also the reputation of a city. Social environmental factors include the values citizens place on certain activities. Countries like Australia are considered sporting nations due to the emphasis and prestige placed on sport. Other countries particularly in Europe and Asia might value science and technology in a higher regard. Thus, the societal norms affecting sport policy need to be taken into consideration. The technological environment includes the information and communications sector, which influences data processing speed. Increasingly, social media and other mobile communications are being used in sport so it is important that sport policy considers these factors.

Sport policy is the key tool that will enable the right use of resources that promote entrepreneurship. There is no right policy for social entrepreneurship; rather, it depends on the human elements that form part of the entrepreneurship experience. Social entrepreneurship in sport has been used as a way to focus on social issues that include diversity management. There are under-represented groups of society that can be helped when sports clubs take an interest in them. This includes encouraging participation in sport-related activities such as business ventures. Due to the rising interest in migration and immigration in society, sport serves as a way to promote peace and harmony in the environment. This has led to sport for development being a way to facilitate a link between sport and under-represented communities.

Promoting social equality in developing countries through sport programs has been initiated in many sports clubs. In order to conduct social entrepreneurship there needs to be appropriate financial arrangements. Social financing is part of this process as it focuses on placing capital in investments perceived as having a social good. Sometimes referred to as impact investing, social financing enables market mechanisms to be used for social causes. Allocating capital to causes that have a societal impact can help channel funds into social entrepreneurship. Social finance is defined as "a mode of managing financial capital for social and environmental benefits" (Moore and Westley, 2012:185). There are different ways that finance can have a social goal, including through impact investing and philanthropic endeavors. The way finance is perceived as being social is related to its mission statement and types of investment.

Social enterprises are often run by people who have a specific cause they are interested in and this links with the aims and objectives of the business. This is referred to as mission-related impact as the social enterprise is governed by social goals in addition to commercial purposes. Social enterprises need protective spaces that enable creativity and experimentation to help refine ideas before entering the market. These protective spaces enable a supportive environment to emerge that facilitates dynamic interaction amongst multiple stakeholders. By focusing on novel ideas that are likely to bring social gains, the protective space can help build positive engagement. This helps build knowledge exchanges between various stakeholders and provide access to ideas. Networks of individuals and organizations in these stakeholder relationships enable social visions to emerge. This encourages thoughts around the types of social enterprise expectations that can be shared and articulated to stakeholders.

Need for new thinking

Many sports organizations have been in existence for a long time and are considered by some to be outdated and bureaucratic. However, this is not always the case as sports organizations can still be entrepreneurial despite their age. Rather than being backward organizations there are many sports organizations that value entrepreneurship and have practices in place to encourage this form of behavior. To move forward with new business practices, it is essential that sports organizations take a collaborative stance towards entrepreneurship. The literature on social entrepreneurship in sport is sparse, thus reflecting the newness of the research area. This has resulted in the importance of social entrepreneurship in sport not being fundamentally discussed in the literature as it presupposes that industry context is not relevant. This is in line with general research on social entrepreneurship, which focuses more on generalizations than specific contexts.

There are a number of steps required to integrate social entrepreneurship into sport including prioritizing, transforming and relating. The prioritization stage involves establishing social entrepreneurship as a key activity that can distinguish sports organizations as socially minded. Sports organizations can do this by establishing social value as part of their civic duties and encourage athletes to be involved in these activities. As athletes are considered role models in society, having them involved in social ventures can have good marketing effects. The transforming stage involves influencing organizational practices that involve social entrepreneurship. This can include athletes embarking on projects that have an intrinsic social value. The relating stage means discussing the role social entrepreneurship plays in sport and how it can affect performance. This means seeing if any changes are needed in order to have a more social entrepreneurship perspective. It might be cost-effective for sports organizations to partner with non-profit entities in order to help them in the initial stages. The ultimate goal for sports organizations involved in social entrepreneurship may be to start new ventures that have a social goal. There is no exact science to social entrepreneurship as it rather depends on the thoughts and feelings of those involved.

Sports organizations have changed substantially as they have merged into businesses with different customers and product categories. The digital age has further transformed sports organizations who now offer multiple services. This partly explains their decision to be more entrepreneurial and affects their knowledge management techniques. Due to the complex management dynamics of sports organizations, it can be hard to decipher how they engage in entrepreneurship. In addition, with the increasingly borderless global environment, sports organizations now compete against a range of service providers. This makes the conversion of entrepreneurship a must for their global competitiveness. The appearance of being an entrepreneurial organization is important, especially when time is of the essence in introducing new product discoveries.

There is growing inequality in society amongst the rich and the poor, which is influencing the rise in the use of social entrepreneurship. Due to this income inequality there is a need to provide services to those less privileged. At the same time there has been an increased awareness of environmental and social issues such as global warming. More people are thus inclined to partake in consumption habits that have a social goal embedded in the product or service. As Mahto et al. (2018:1) assert, "in the United States the top wealthiest 1% own 40% of the nation's wealth while the bottom 80% own only 7% of the nation's wealth." Social entrepreneurship in a way acts to reallocate wealth by providing essential services to those in need.

Innovators can be individuals, teams or firms (Mahto et al., 2019). From a consumer behavior standpoint, individuals are the main unit of analysis in innovation studies. The ability–motivation–opportunity (AMO) framework is a way to understand individual performance (Englert and Helmig, 2018). Ability refers to the physical and psychological traits that influence the way an individual behaves in the environment. Physical ability includes health and energy levels which impact the way an individual conducts their behavior. In sport these physical abilities can be required to play certain games. Physical characteristics such as height are important in sports such as basketball as it provides a competitive advantage. In other sports such as gymnastics, height can be a disadvantage due to the need for acrobatic activity. Age is another factor that can impact the type of sport played. In the United States there are age restrictions on professional sports such as football. Motor skills also represent a physical attribute that can be developed but are often part of an individual's natural talents.

Motivation refers to the willingness of an individual to perform an action. Some people are more motivated than others and this impacts on their ability to be athletes. Due to the long hours spent in training and development in sport, individuals with more motivation are also more likely to succeed. Motivation can be based on an individual's intrinsic goals that impact on the way they behave or on external factors such as financial benefits. Thus, monetary gain from performing in a good way will impact on an individual's intention to be an athlete. The level of motivation depends on the requirements of the sport with some preferring to play sport for recreational reasons. This results in less emphasis on performance compared to others but is based on enjoyment and socialization. Some sports have specific characteristics that are team- or individual-based that impact motivation levels. Team sports require a group of people to work together for a common goal. This means motivating all members of a team and having team cohesion. Individual sports might involve a need for more psychological motivation due to the isolation and not being part of a team. Thus, there can be personality traits associated with individual sports. Opportunity refers to the environmental context, which can help or hinder performance. In sport there are opportunities that enable an individual to have a better performance than others, such as their position in a race. Alternatively, the conduct of an individual in terms of playing well in a team environment can increase overall performance. Thus, by leveraging the available resources at hand an individual can make the best of their environment.

New theories

In order to address issues pertaining to sport management it is important to develop new theories (Brandon-Lai et al., 2016). This means building on the work from other disciplines by adapting and extending them to a sport context. Establishing new theories is important for the sport management discipline as it has tended to borrow from other fields' already existing theories. As Cunningham (2013:1) states, theories help understand "how, when, why and under what conditions phenomena take place." Theories can refer to a set of relationships or how phenomena evolve in an environmental context. In addition, there is a range of ways theories develop from associating events to certain constructs to establishing the likelihood of an event taking place. This means theories are important to the sport management discipline to advance and progress its impact. As sport management involves the combination of multiple disciplines it seems relevant that additional theories are required to take into account new societal advancements. This enables enlisting different ways of approaching sport management research that are cognizant of the environmental context.

There are a number of behavioral models that have been used to study intentions. Attitude formation is an important topic in psychology and there is a variety of factors that affect attitude. The technology acceptance model has been widely used in research to understand the way individuals perceive technology. Originally developed by Davis (1989) it suggests that perceived usefulness, perceived ease of use and user acceptance are important variables in assessing an individual's acceptance of a new technology.

This classical model was pivotal in understanding the use of emerging technologies made possible by the Internet revolution. As the resulting effects of Internet technologies on performance and productivity were initially unknown, this theory provided a way to determine individuals' intention to use the technology. Whilst actual use is different to intention to use, the perceptions of a technology in terms of ease of use are useful to know. The initial theory has been extended to other contexts as technological innovation has progressed. As sport is a social phenomenon requiring interaction amongst participants, the technology acceptance model can be used to understand the use of new innovations such as virtual reality. The idea of having a theory on social entrepreneurship in sport is to further extend and transform current research. This will potentially lead to a new theory being used in sport that takes a transdisciplinary approach to social entrepreneurship.

References

Arco-Castro, L., López-Pérez, M. V., Pérez-López, M. C. and Rodríguez-Ariza, L. (2018) "Corporate philanthropy and employee engagement," *Review of Managerial Science*, 1–21.

Boris, E. T. and Steuerle, C. E. (2006) "Scope and dimensions of the nonprofit sector," in W. W. Powell and R. Steinberg (eds), *The nonprofit sector: A research handbook* (pp. 66–88). New Haven, CT: Yale University Press.

Brandon-Lai, S. A., Armstrong, C. G. and Ferris, G. R. (2016) "Organisational impression congruence: A conceptual model of multi-level impression management operation in sports service organisations," *Sport Management Review*, 19(5): 492–505.

Brinckerhoff, P. C. (1995) *Mission-based management*. Oak Park, IL: Alpine Guild.

Cunningham, G. B. (2013) "Theory and theory development in sport management," *Sport Management Review*, 16(1): 1–4.

Davis, E. (1989) "Perceived usefulness, perceived ease of use and user acceptance of information technologies," *MIS Quarterly*, 13(3): 319–340.

Dennissen, M., Benschop, Y. and Brink, M. (2018) "Rethinking diversity management: An intersectional analysis of diversity networks," *Organization Studies*, 1–22.

Dyllick, T. and Hockerts, K. (2002) "Beyond the business case for corporate sustainability," *Business Strategy and the Environment*, 11(2): 130–141.

Englert, B. and Helmig, B. (2018) "Volunteer performance in the light of organizational success: A systematic literature review," *Voluntas*, 29: 1–28.

Ferreira, J. and Ratten, V. (2018) "Competitiveness of locations: The effects of regional innovation and entrepreneurial practices," *Competitiveness Review: An International Business Journal Incorporating Journal of Global Competitiveness*, 28(1): 2–5.

Ferreira, J. J., Fernandes, C. I. and Ratten, V. (2017) "Entrepreneurship, innovation and competitiveness: What is the connection?" *International Journal of Business and Globalisation*, 18(1): 73–95.

Fortunato, M. (2014) "Supporting rural entrepreneurship: A review of conceptual development from research to practice," *Community Development*, 45(4): 387–408.

Kim, E., Fredline, L. and Cuskelly, G. (2018) "Heterogeneity of sport event volunteer motivations: A segmentation approach," *Tourism Management*, 68: 375–386.

Mahto, R., Belousova, O. and Ahluwaha, S. (2019) "Abundance – A new window on how disruptive innovation occurs," *Technological Forecasting & Social Change*, in press.

Moore M. L. and Westley F. (2012) "The social finance and social innovation nexus," *Journal of Social Entrepreneurship*, 3(2): 115–132.

Morris, M., Neumeyer, X., Jang, Y. and Kuratko, D. (2018) "Distinguishing types of entrepreneurial ventures: An identity-based perspective," *Journal of Small Business Management*, 56(3): 453–474.

Mota, A., Braga, V. and Ratten, V. (2019) "Entrepreneurship motivation: Opportunity and necessity," in V. Ratten, P. Jones, V. Braga and C. Marques (eds), *Sustainable entrepreneurship* (pp. 139–165). Cham: Springer.

Peterson, D. (2018) "Enhancing corporate reputation through corporate philanthropy," *Journal of Strategy and Management*, 11(1): 18–32.

Ratten, V. (2019) *Frugal innovation*. London: Routledge.

Ratten, V. and Tajeddini, K. (2019) "Entrepreneurship and sport business research, synthesis and lessons: Introduction to the special journal issue," *International Journal of Sport Management and Marketing*, 19(1/2): 1–7.

Rinkinen, S., Oikarinen, T. and Melkas, H. (2016) "Social enterprises in regional innovation systems: A review of Finnish regional strategies," *European Planning Studies*, 24, 723–741.

Ryan, R. M. and Deci, E. L. (2000) "Self-determination theory and the facilitation of intrinsic motivation, social development, and well-being," *American Psychologist*, 55: 68–78.

Stromquist, N. P. (1998) "NGOs in a new paradigm of civil society," *Current Issues in Comparative Education*, 1(1): 1–5.

Welty Peachey, J., Burton, L., Wells, J. and Chung, M. R. (2018) "Exploring servant leadership and needs satisfaction in the sport for development and peace context," *Journal of Sport Management*, 32(2): 96–108.

Will, M., Roth, S. and Valentinov, V. (2018) "From non-profit diversity to organizational multifunctionality: A systems-theoretical proposal," *Administration & Society*, 50(7): 1015–1036.

Zietlow, J. (2001) "Social entrepreneurship: Management, finance and marketing aspects," *Journal of Nonprofit & Public Sector Marketing*, 9(1–2): 19–43.

6

GENDER AND SOCIAL ENTREPRENEURSHIP IN SPORT

Introduction

The word "entrepreneur" has an assumed meaning of acting in a self-interested way by pursuing financial objectives. Schumpeter (1939:82) described entrepreneurs in grandiose terms by stating they had "super normal qualities of intellect and will." This stereotype of entrepreneurs as having above average intelligence is perpetuated in the literature but in reality, this intelligence may be the result of life experience rather than a formal education (Ferreira et al., 2018). This means that intellect can be in the form of business knowledge, perseverance and persistence. When an individual has both qualities and a capacity for innovation, they are considered to be good entrepreneurs. Entrepreneurs have been considered as extroverts due to their need to persist in times of hardship and market themselves. Extraversion is defined as "the tendency to be assertive, enjoy the company of other people and large groups, and seek excitement and stimulation" (Zhang et al., 2009:90). This perception has changed with some famous entrepreneurs being considered introverts and the power of being quiet is now considered an entrepreneurial attribute.

Entrepreneurship can be considered from an economic or social point of view (Humbert and Drew, 2010). The economic perspective has been the dominant school of thought until recently when the social perspective gained popularity (Ratten et al., 2017). In the economic perspective, money is the main consideration in terms of financial output. Thus, economists tend to downplay societal and personality facts that affect entrepreneurship and overemphasize financial concerns. The social perspective of entrepreneurship takes a broader view of entrepreneurship by acknowledging other pertinent factors such as gender, socio-demographics and family experience in affecting entrepreneurship. Gender is important in social relations and has become more used in entrepreneurship research. Elam (2008) suggested that there are multiple ways of analyzing the relationship between gender and entrepreneurship, which includes the individual, family and societal point of view, although each of these dimensions has an economic or social point of view.

The economic and social schools of thought need to be considered in terms of enterprise spirit and motivations. Most individuals or organizations are motivated by a combination of push or pull factors. The push factors affecting entrepreneurship are "elements that drive people into entrepreneurship such as the need for greater income or dissatisfaction within the labour market" (Humbert and Drew, 2010:177). These push factors normally take an economic point of view, making the decision to be an entrepreneur a necessity rather than a choice. The pull factors involve "elements that induce people to become entrepreneurs, such as the desire for autonomy and independence, the wish, rather than the need for a greater income, the desire for personal satisfaction and achievement" (Humbert and Drew, 2010:177). There has been more interest in entrepreneurship as a career due to both the autonomy it provides and the greater control over work/life balance it enables.

Only recently has the term "social entrepreneur" become popular although the idea has been around for a long time. The combination of the words "social" and "entrepreneur" are interesting as it implies that business activities can have a societal benefit. Bruni et al. (2004:408) assert that "entrepreneurship is historically located in the symbolic universe of the male." This is reflected in the type of business activity associated with entrepreneurs being corporate based. Whilst there are many entrepreneurs who have small businesses, typically the emphasis has been on large businesses that have global appeal (Langowitz and Minniti, 2007). Successful entrepreneurs can have small or large-sized businesses but normally the bigger the business the more likely the link to success (Ratten, 2012). However, success means different things to different people depending on their attitudes. For some, having a business that provides a certain level of income is equated with success but for others success means international recognition. In addition, the born global firms that start exporting soon after inception have become more dominant in the literature, reflecting the ability of small firms to also compete with large firms. This is particularly evident in the sports industry, which has focused on internationalization for increased performance outcomes.

The profile of female athletes has risen over the past decade with greater emphasis on gender equality. At the same time there has been a surge of interest in social entrepreneurship, which combines profit and non-profit interests (Miragaia et al., 2017). The combination of gender and social entrepreneurship in sport has yet to be fully explored in the literature although it exists in practice. Whilst female athletes have more global recognition, there are still some gender disparities in sport, from the way female athletes manage their careers to how they engage with stakeholders. Traditionally social entrepreneurship has been viewed as a more feminine form of entrepreneurship due to its emphasis on volunteer management and philanthropy. In the past, females conducted social activities at sport events in support of male professional athletes. Whilst this has somewhat changed there is still a tendency to view social entrepreneurship as a gendered activity. However, there may be some gender differences in behavior that are worth exploring in a sport context. The aim of this chapter is to review the literature on social entrepreneurship in sport by focusing on women's entrepreneurship. This will move forward our thinking about how gender affects sport by stressing the importance of social activities. The chapter starts with a discussion about women's entrepreneurship and the place gender has in the sports industry. It then progresses into an examination of gender in social sport ventures before concluding with some future research ideas and managerial implications.

Women's entrepreneurship

Entrepreneurship is generally viewed as the study of business opportunities, which can occur in a number of contexts including the sport realm. Recognizing opportunities is at the heart of entrepreneurship as it represents the most distinctive way to assess entrepreneurship (Noguera et al., 2013). Anderson (2008:395) asserts how "entrepreneurship itself remains a deeply gendered institution, and how that is constructed through everyday practice rooted in space and place." Gender studies has a long history in business management literature but many of the studies originated in the anthropology field (Ranga and Etzkowitz, 2010). This is due to the reality and experiences of women being pertinent to understanding their position in society. Social anthropology is a useful way to understand the role of gender and entrepreneurship in sport (Ratten, 2011). Gender has been a key component of anthropology studies and the sport management discipline can gain from the extant anthropology literature. Sanday (1973) produced an influential article suggesting a theory about the status of women and suggested that women's position in society differs globally depending on the culture. This was in contrast to the prevailing view at the time that women were treated the same everywhere due to their gender.

Sanday (1973) stated that there were geographical and cultural conditions affecting the status of women. This meant in some society's women had a higher power status than men and were not naturally submissive, which was the dominant belief. This questioned the prevailing myths and stereotypes of women in terms of their behavior in society. Another seminal anthropological study was conducted by Richards (1956) who investigated the initiation ceremony of females into an African community and found that gender is learnt rather than being solely a biological fact. This means that much of the behavior we associate with gender is socially constructed based on societal norms. This is reflected in Bullough et al. (2017:216) who state that "femininity is associated with nature, emotion, rawness, childhood, and so forth, while masculinity is associated with culture, reason, crookedness, adulthood." These gender characteristics have been perpetuated in the literature and in society. As Ardener (1975) suggested, women are a group of society who express themselves through common cultural connections. This means society gives different groups preference based on institutional pressures. Women as a group of society are reliant on how they interact with social obligations and political considerations.

Women's attitudes towards entrepreneurship can be centered on the micro, meso and macro perspectives (De Bruin et al., 2007). The micro perspective focuses on the household or family context. It takes a narrow view in terms of women's behavior being influenced by motherhood or other family-related factors. This is evident in Rossi (1965:1201) stating that women in top science positions have "extraordinary motivation, thick skins, exceptional ability and some unusual pattern of socialization." A broader perspective is the meso view, which acknowledges the role of the environment in terms of institutions and structures. This means women develop their entrepreneurial capabilities through being involved in social networks, which are also used in conjunction with environmental factors. As Hanson (2009:249) states, "gender always intersects with other axes of difference, such as age, ethnicity, race or class." The macro view suggests that cultural conditions in terms of behavioral norms impact entrepreneurship. This means that governments can introduce strategies to harness the entrepreneurial potential of women.

The term "women's work" has been typically used as a derogatory term to describe jobs that are considered gender-based. This has created some irritation amongst individuals who enjoy doing certain tasks because of a sense of self-fulfillment. In the past, some occupations were only available to women and they normally involved the service or manufacturing professions. The sense of caring was associated with women's duties and this was reflected in gender relations. Regardless of one's view about the role of women in the workforce, there are some lagging stereotypes. This is seen in the way women behave and is reflected in the number of females in sport management positions.

Women tend to have a different socialization process compared to men, which is the result of their upbringing or environmental context. Baron et al. (2001) suggest that women value entrepreneurship as less desirable than men. This means that women can be less attuned to possibilities in the marketplace. Another view is that women are not presented with opportunities because entrepreneurship is considered a male activity (Nilsson, 1997). Thus, society can tend to focus more on male business leaders than on females.

Gregory (1990) suggested that there are three main theoretical perspectives to understanding gender: person, organization and gender context. The person-centered perspective focuses on how individual characteristics such as level of motivation affect business performance. The organization-centered view suggests that a person's position in the corporate hierarchy reflects how they behave. People in higher levels of authority will act in a different way to those in a subordinate position. The gender-centered perspective relies on biological characteristics that impact social status. This includes the way females dress and act in society.

Smith (2015:256) states "in western societies, men are hero figures hyped by the myth-making process associated with the cult of the entrepreneur." Thus, in global society, men have been assumed to be the entrepreneurs and women in more supportive roles. This has changed but there is still a predominance of male entrepreneur seen in the media that makes this stereotype continue. Whilst the myth of all entrepreneurs being men is untrue, changing societal attitudes towards women entrepreneurs have made people rethink the role of entrepreneurship in society. Entrepreneurs are not always lone heroes but can be part of a partnership or group of people. This is referred to as copreneurship as there are a number of people cooperating in an entrepreneurial endeavor. Smith (2014: 256) states that copreneurship is a "genuine power-sharing model feeding upon personal needs, complementary skills, shared histories, dreams and values." Copreneurship works well in a number of business contexts but particularly in the sport context due to the large number of public/private partnerships.

Language is a way that entrepreneurship has been considered to be a masculine pursuit. This is evident in Collins and Moore (1964:5) in discussing entrepreneurs, stating that "he emerges as essentially more masculine than feminine, more heroic than cowardly." This emphasis on the male pronoun in using the word entrepreneur is repeated in much of the entrepreneurship literature. This may not be specifically related to entrepreneurship, however, as the male pronoun was used by many researchers in the past when referring to business people. There is now an emphasis on gender neutrality in research, which can lessen the effect of gender connotations in entrepreneurship studies.

Entrepreneurs are assumed to be competitive and have the physical capacity to work constantly (Bruni et al., 2004). These characteristics have been associated with males due to the emphasis on strength. More recently other interpretations of entrepreneurs have emerged in the literature. In addition, the recognition that all males do not have the same attributes has been acknowledged. Whilst gender influences entrepreneurship, there are differing views about its impact. Gender plays a role in the historical development of entrepreneurship research with famous entrepreneurs such as Henry Ford and Andrew Carnegie being male. In addition, the founders of sport companies like Adidas and Nike were male, further reflecting the tendency to emphasize males in sport management.

How a gender view of sport and social entrepreneurship contributes to the literature

Sport entrepreneurs express their entrepreneurial behavior by recognizing opportunities that others have not seen. This means sport entrepreneurs act on opportunities in a way that managers do not. Public organizations involved in sport and gender policy have highlighted their interest in women sport entrepreneurs. This is due to sport having long been focused on male professional leagues with football being the world's most popular sport, although women's participation in football has increased and there is more emphasis on female sports in general. In some sports, like tennis, there has been equal pay for men and women for some time. Other sports like surfing have followed this trend by offering equal pay regardless of gender. In the United States, Title IX has meant equal funding to male and female college sports.

Gender studies is a well-researched topic in sport management but more emphasis by policymakers has been made on women's participation in sport and entrepreneurship. Early studies that examined why there are few women in science suggested that it was due to a lack of confidence. Sports organizations need to focus their energies on adopting social forms of entrepreneurship within their business strategy. For social entrepreneurship to occur it needs to go through a number of stages from having the right mindset, process, then outcome. In the initial stages there may be an improvised solution towards how social entrepreneurship emerges in a sports organization. This is due to the need for organizational learning to occur and changes made to suit the social business practices. Some organizations might find it easy to balance their for-profit and non-profit business initiatives, but this depends on the situation.

Clever sports organizations that realize the potential of social entrepreneurship are able to incorporate it in a more efficient manner. This helps increase the level of innovation by focusing on ingenuity. To do this the implementation of new ideas regarding social issues needs to be integrated into existing business practices. This helps with sports organizations enhancing both their economic and social well-being. To create further opportunities regarding social entrepreneurship it is important that sports organizations think about the right way to incorporate social change. This can occur by having more inclusive innovation practices regarding social entrepreneurship. Sports organizations need to create new routines for social entrepreneurship that, whilst based on existing ones, have a social component. This can mean applying resources to solve social problems in a new way. Different combinations of resources may be needed depending on the sustainability of the solution to the social problem.

The process of implementing social entrepreneurship into a sports organization involves approaching social issues in a way that creates value. This enables time and resource efficiency in achieving a good outcome for a sports organization. Some of the ways to do this involve focusing on service ecosystems that mean the social entrepreneurship can be transferred to other contexts. The outcome for sports organizations from social entrepreneurship can include different types of innovation such as disruptive or incremental. Major changes in how sports organizations see social opportunities will result in disruptive innovations that impact the sports industry. This means that social change has an impact on the current level of services. Incremental innovation means less change as it focuses on smaller alterations to a sports organization's strategy.

Bricolage is a process used to describe doing something with the resources that are available and can involve incremental forms of innovation. Increasingly, it has been used in an entrepreneurship context to describe the way entrepreneurs make the best out of their environmental situation. There will not always be the appropriate amount or type of resources available, so taking a bricolage approach is useful. Bricolage entrepreneurs are defined as "those who solve a problem or create an opportunity by applying combinations of the resources available" (Soni and Krishnan, 2014:32). The notion of bricolage entrepreneurs has been used more in developed or emerging economies due to the popularity of frugal innovation. Similar to the idea of social entrepreneurship, frugal innovation encapsulates the idea that innovation does not need to be expensive but can be cheaply done with few resources. This relates to social entrepreneurship, as often the resources needed are not available, so sports organizations need to make the best out of what they can do. As time is of the essence for sports organizations, the social entrepreneurship they conduct needs to use resources that are available instead of what is required. This means the process of social entrepreneurship is not always perfect but, rather, the action or behavior constitutes good behavior. This relates to the entrepreneurship process of effectuation. Soni and Krishnan (2014:32) define effectuation as "where the innovator or entrepreneur does not intend to predict the future but instead manages the contingencies with the available resources." This is a realistic approach and useful in the context of social entrepreneurship in sports organizations.

Policies for shaping more female participation in social entrepreneurship

At the start of this chapter, I highlighted how there is little research about the role gender plays in social entrepreneurship. This lack of alignment particularly regarding female entrepreneurs' participation in social ventures is surprising given the stereotype of non-profit activities being dominated by females. Whilst there has been more emphasis on females in sport, there are still new policy directions needed. This will help produce better guidelines for the way sports organizations manage gender diversity in sport.

There need to be more incentives for females to participate in sport social entre-preneurship, from producing ideas to implementing strategies. Social entrepreneur-ship has a wide societal implication but its application in the sports industry is still nascent. A simplification of how to conduct sport social entrepreneurship would enable more females to be involved. This can help both the social venture and sports organization in achieving gender equality. This relates to social entrepre-neurship in sport as it is considered more of a choice and opportunity than a need. Therefore, social entrepreneurs in sport have a journey of entrepreneurial awakening based on personal factors. This might include sport for development or helping people engage in sport in less-developed countries. Alternatively, it could include using sport as a way to affect cultural relations in society and to bring about gender equality. Research on gender and sport seems to be compartmentalized and not linked to other areas. This has resulted in the role of gender in sport social enterprises being under-represented despite its cultural significance. Whilst it is dif-ficult to see the connections between gender, sport and social entrepreneurship, they are important and can yield interesting findings.

Sport has traditionally been viewed as a more masculine activity due to the emphasis on competition. In addition, physical traits such as strength that are associated with males are needed in sport. In the past decade, more feminine qual-ities in sport have been acknowledged, such as quietness and contemplation that can be as a result of societal changes but also different forms of sport such as yoga becoming more popular. Social entrepreneurship has both masculine and feminine traits. Camaraderie and teamwork are important in sport but have had a tradition of being associated with male sports, such as football. Social entrepreneurship needs these skills as, by definition, the social part of the word involves collaboration. As there are different forms of teamwork in sport from the playing field to coaching and support activities it makes sense that sport teams would also be good at social entrepreneurship. Feminine traits such as nurturing and caring are evident in sport but depend on the context. Sport teams need a range of people, including physiotherapists and psychologists, who can focus on support activities. Whilst the emphasis in sport is on winning, teamwork and collaboration in sport can also be applied to social entrepreneurship activities.

The sport ethic is influenced by men's social expectations about behavior (Berg et al., 2014). Sports like football are viewed as expressions of masculinity in terms of playing styles and attitudes to competition (Fogel, 2011). This results in behaviors in sport that have masculine characteristics being viewed as acceptable. Society views athletes in high regard so the behavior on the playing field is evaluated in other parts of society. The male traits shown on the sporting field, such as aggression and dominance, are viewed as positive also in business. This means athletes are also considered as natural business people due to their ability to be competitive. The stoicism in the face of pain shown by athletes is considered a male trait. This contrasts with females who are considered too emotional to behave in a rational manner (Berg et al., 2014). These gender differences are embodied in everyday practices and result in continued inequality.

The inequalities and risks associated with sport are also evident in entrepreneurs. Whilst risk is a part of any sport, some risks can be calculated more than others. This is due to the rules governing sport. It can be hard to change existing cultural practices in sport due to the need to adhere to already existing guidelines. This makes any alternative way of playing sport an area for policy improvement. Women in sport have been viewed as weak and not able to have the same stamina as men. This is perpetuated in sports. Masculinity is evident in football, which emphasizes physical ability. Football players who are injured in the course of the game or are in pain but struggle on regardless are considered to be good athletes. Theberge (2008) suggested that being injured is expected for professional athletes in terms of taking one for the team. This connection with injury and team bonding is another way masculinity is connected to sport. In team sports, the camaraderie from being part of a group is an important social element of sport. As Fogel (2011:12) states, "football remains as one of the last spaces in the sports coliseum. As such, the popularity of football rests largely on the glorification of male superiority." More females are playing football but it will take some time before there is gender equity.

Gender can also be examined from a social responsibility point of view. Smith and Westerbeek (2007) suggest that there are ten main ways that social responsibility is a unique feature of sport: rules, safety, independence, transparency, pathways, community relations, health, environment, developmental focus and coaching. Each different type of sport has its own rules, which govern how to play the game. Rules ensure that there is a consistent form of behavior across games. This helps maintain standards and compare performance rates across multiple games. Rules ensure equality between games but also enable people access to the game. This can help increase diversity as players are assessed based on their performance rather than any personal attributes. Sport for all is a mantra of many government policy initiatives and helps increase the number of females in sport. Safety refers to being socially responsible for what occurs on and off the playing field. It is important that the actions of individuals in a sport are considered in terms of their impact on society. This includes having appropriate safety equipment that protects both athletes and spectators. In nature-based sports, it may be difficult to ensure the safety of competitors so having guidelines in place can help. In addition, there is the health and physical safety of participants that needs to be considered in sport games.

Independence refers to non-bias in decisions in sport. There can be preferential treatment given in sport but a social responsibility perspective ensures a level playing field. This helps to ensure that people with vested interests such as fans or club owners do not interfere with the game. Gambling and illegal betting on games is not allowed when taking a social responsibility perspective. Governance relates to how sport is played and this means having a fair governing body that makes decisions regarding sport. Transparency is an important part of this process, ensuring people receive the same information. As there are many politics in sport, transparency is important in ensuring fairness. This helps build a good reputation for a sport. Pathways for athlete development are useful in ensuring athletes stay committed to a sport. This means mentoring junior players and ensuring that they have a way to transfer from amateur to professional players. To do this, a community relations policy might apply, which ensures sport teams take into account their surrounding environment. The social needs of the local community need to be taken into account along with national and international interests. The health of society at large should be considered when designing sport policy. This involves having different socio-demographic groups participate in sport. Sport teams need to do this by protecting the environment and encouraging sustainable initiatives such as the use of renewable energy. Ensuring playing fields are maintained and developed are policies needed to formalize this commitment. In addition, there needs to be transformational leaders who can implement social change in sports.

Ways forward

There are three main tasks needed to advance the gender, sport and social entrepreneurship literature. First, gender needs to be considered as a fluid and dynamic concept that is shaped by society. It is a biological concept but social relationships affect its development. This means that power and political relationships in sport need to be considered. Thus gender, whilst based on masculinity and femininity, is also impacted by sport practices. The experiences of females in sport need to be considered when discussing social entrepreneurship.

Second, the context of social entrepreneurship in sport needs to be evaluated. There is a range of different ways sport can utilize social entrepreneurship so the social dimensions in these practices need to be discussed. Therefore, the marketing, product development or service delivery should be analyzed in terms of how this impacts gender relations. Some people interpret differently social entrepreneurship so there needs to be some form of reference. This involves emphasizing the way social entrepreneurship in sport can bring benefits such as increased social cohesion or diversity.

Third, the digital impact of social entrepreneurship in sport needs to be highlighted. Due to increased usage of social media, more digital forms of social entrepreneurship can apply in sport, for example, online sites or lobbying efforts around social issues that sports organizations can participate in. In the social entrepreneurship literature, the focus is on the social element of entrepreneurship as compared to the effect of gender. This means that there are few studies, particularly in a sport context, that focus on gender roles in social entrepreneurship. Women entrepreneurs, like female athletes, sometimes are in the minority although there is considerable variation depending on the context. Some sports have more female than male athletes such as netball and softball. These sports were started as softer alternatives to basketball and baseball, which only males tended to play, and have different playing styles.

There is still a need to have different sports for specific genders, but this is changing with a trend towards gender-neutral sports. As Welsh and Kaciak (2019:1) state, "work and family are intertwined areas of life for most people but they [are] especially connected for entrepreneurs." Entrepreneurship whilst always having been a part of the sports industry has been discussed more in recent years due to increased technological innovations. Social entrepreneurship usually involves more low-tech products and services, although it can have a high-tech component in some circumstances. This is evident in online sport gaming communities organizing social business ventures for those in need.

Conclusion

There are four main outcomes regarding the use of gender and social entrepreneurship in sport: recognition, attitude, patronage and satisfaction. Recognition involves the acknowledgement that there are social issues that the sports industry can help fix. Sensitive issues such as the participation of females in sport can be addressed through gender equity programs. This enables the recognition of the gender imbalance in some sports and how entrepreneurship can be used as a catalyst for social change. Attitude reflects the way people perceive a social issue and how they deal with it. In the past females were not allowed to play certain sports, so changing attitudes towards female players can help create social change. Patronage involves the number of people paying attention to a certain social issue. This can include purchasing rates or participation in social ventures. Satisfaction refers to the emotions an individual feels from being involved in sport. For some, being involved in not-for-profit initiatives or being a volunteer is important for them.

References

Anderson, E. (2008) "Whose name's on the awning? Gender, entrepreneurship and the American diner," *Gender, Place & Culture*, 15(4): 395–410.

Ardener, S. (ed.) (1975) "Introduction," to *Perceiving Women*. New York: Wiley and Sons.

Baron, R. A., Markman, G. D. and Hirsa, A. (2001) "Perceptions of women and men as entrepreneurs: Evidence for differential effects of attributional augmenting," *Journal of Applied Psychology*, 86(5): 923.

Berg, E. C., Migliaccio, T. A. and Anzini-Varesio, R. (2014) "Female football players, the sport ethic and the masculinity–sport nexus," *Sport in Society*, 17(2): 176–189.

Bruni, A., Gherardi, S. and Poggio, B. (2004) "Doing gender, doing entrepreneurship: An ethnographic account of intertwined practices," *Gender, Work and Organization*, 11(4): 406–429.

Bullough, A., Renko, M. and Abdelzaher, D. (2017) "Women's business ownership: Operating within the context of institutional and in-group collectivism," *Journal of Management*, 43(7): 2037–2064.

Collins, O. and Moore, D. (1964) *The enterprising man*. East Lansing, MI: Michigan State University Press.

De Bruin, A., Brush, C. and Welter, F. (2007) "Advancing a framework for coherent research on women's entrepreneurship," *Entrepreneurship Theory and Practice*, 31(3): 323–339.

Elam, A. (2008) *Gender and entrepreneurship: A multilevel theory and analysis*. London: Edward Elgar Publishing.

Ferreira, J. J., Fayolle, A., Ratten, V. and Raposo, M. (eds) (2018) *Entrepreneurial universities*. Cheltenham: Edward Elgar Publishing.

Fogel, C. (2011) "Sporting masculinity on the gridiron: Construction, characteristics and consequences," *Canadian Social Science*, 7(2): 1–14.

Gregory, A. (1990) "Are women different and are women thought to be different? Theoretical and methodological perspectives," *Journal of Business Ethics*, 9: 257–266.

Hanson, S. (2009) "Changing places through women's entrepreneurship," *Economic Geography*, 85(3): 245–267.

Humbert, A. and Drew, E. (2010) "Gender, entrepreneurship and motivational factors in an Irish context," *International Journal of Gender and Entrepreneurship*, 2(2): 173–196.

Langowitz, N. and Minniti, M. (2007) "The entrepreneurial propensity of women," *Entrepreneurship Theory and Practice*, 31: 341–364.

Miragaia, D. A., Ferreira, J. and Ratten, V. (2017) "Corporate social responsibility and social entrepreneurship: Drivers of sports sponsorship policy," *International Journal of Sport Policy and Politics*, 9(4): 613–623.

Nilsson, P. (1997) "Business counselling services directed towards female entrepreneurs – some legitimacy dilemmas," *Entrepreneurship and Regional Development*, 9(3): 239–258.

Noguera, M., Alvarez, C. and Urbano, D. (2013) "Socio-cultural factors and female entrepreneurship," *International Entrepreneurship and Management Journal*, 9: 183–197.

Ranga, M. and Etzkowitz, H. (2010) "Athena in the world of techne: The gender dimension of technology, innovation and entrepreneurship," *Journal of Technology Management & Innovation*, 5(1): 1–12.

Ratten, V. (2011) "A social perspective of sports-based entrepreneurship," *International Journal of Entrepreneurship and Small Business*, 12(3): 314–326.

Ratten, V. (2012) "Entrepreneurship, e-finance and mobile banking," *International Journal of Electronic Finance*, 6(1): 1–12.

Ratten, V., Ferreira, J. J. and Fernandes, C. I. (2017) "Innovation management: Current trends and future directions," *International Journal of Innovation and Learning*, 22(2): 135–155.

Richards, A. I. (1956) *Chisungu: A girls' initiation ceremony among the Bemba of Northern Rhodesia* (Vol. 3). London: Faber & Faber.

Rossi, A. (1965) "Women in science: Why so few?" *Science*, 148: 1196–1203.

Sanday, P. R. (1973) "Toward a theory of the status of women," *American Anthropologist*, 75(5): 1682–1700.

Schumpeter, J. (1939) *Business cycles: A theoretical, historical and statistical analysis of the capitalist process*. New York: McGraw-Hill.

Smith, A. and Westerbeek, H. (2007) "Sport as a vehicle for deploying corporate social responsibility," *Journal of Corporate Citizenship*, 1–12.

Smith, R. (2014) "Assessing the contribution of the 'theory of matriarchy' to the entrepreneurship and family business literatures," *International Journal of Gender and Entrepreneurship*, 6(3): 255–275.

Soni, P. and Krishnan, R. (2014) "Frugal innovation: Aligning theory, practice, and public policy," *Journal of Indian Business Research*, 6(1): 29–47.

Theberge, N. (2008) "'Just a normal bad part of what I do': Elite athletes' accounts of the relationship between health and sport," *Sociology of Sport Journal*, 25(2): 206–222.

Welsh, D. H. and Kaciak, E. (2019) "Family enrichment and women entrepreneurial success: The mediating effect of family interference," *International Entrepreneurship and Management Journal*, in press, 1–31.

Zhang, Z., Zyphur, M., Narayanan, J., Arvey, R., Chaturvedi, S., Avolio, B., Lichtenstein, P. and Larsson, G. (2009) "The genetic basis of entrepreneurship: Effects of gender and personality," *Organizational Behavior and Human Decision Processes*, 110: 93–1087.

7

THE FUTURE OF SOCIAL ENTREPRENEURSHIP IN SPORT

Introduction

This book contributes to the research dialogue on social entrepreneurship by identifying some factors influencing sport-based social entrepreneurship. In particular, I have stressed the importance of building more social enterprises in sport. Having a more detailed commitment to social entrepreneurship, will, I conclude, be necessary to the evolution of the sports industry. In order to be effective in society, more sports organizations need to become experts in social entrepreneurship. This is why it is so important for more sports organizations to embed a social entrepreneurial spirit within their workplace practices and engage with the community.

Social entrepreneurship, whilst a buzzword ten years ago, is now considered an essential part of society. This has meant the use of the words "social entrepreneurship" to define a wide range of activities without taking into account the intricacies and nuances of each social enterprise. This has resulted in a plethora of general social entrepreneurship studies but there is a knowledge gap in the field of social entrepreneurship in sport. This has been brought about by insufficient research connecting social entrepreneurship to sport, which has impeded the research (Miragaia et al., 2018). Sports organizations are a particular type of actor that needs to be studied separately to other types of organizations. This derives from the fact sports organizations have special characteristics that alter their behavior in terms of allocating resources towards social ventures (Ratten, 2011). Sports organizations interact with their environment differently to other types of organizations due to their embeddedness in the community. The position of sports organizations in a community is a result of geography but also economic, historical and social conditions. Considering the environment for analyzing social entrepreneurship in sport brings a new perspective to the existing literature on sports organizations (Ratten, 2016). Amongst sport entrepreneurship practitioners there is already a strong sense of social entrepreneurship but this needs to be incorporated into more research. This is important as sport is considered both a leisure and a business activity that has influenced its social objectives.

The topic of social entrepreneurship reflects a trend towards more interdisciplinary research in sport management. Tackling complex issues can help to shift the focus from purely sport literature to incorporate other perspectives that have an interdisciplinary perspective. In this book an intriguing question in sport science has been asked: what is the role of social entrepreneurship in stimulating the sports industry? This is a fundamental question that needs to be addressed as more sports organizations become involved in social ventures (Ratten, 2017). Answering this question will enable the sports industry to design better forms of social ventures that can increase societal well-being.

This chapter has the following structure. First, I discuss an overview of the topic of social entrepreneurship in sport as a way to understand the main contributions of the book. Second, I discuss how there needs to be more research using the theoretical framework of sport and social entrepreneurship that has been reviewed in this book. Third, an outlook for future research on social entrepreneurship in sport is provided that includes research gaps and trends. In conclusion, I elaborate on the complexities of social entrepreneurship and how the sports industry is in a unique position to deal with these challenges. The likely practical implications of research into sport and social entrepreneurship, which highlight its eminent importance, are addressed.

Richness of social entrepreneurship in sport

There is expected to be a deluge of research studies on social entrepreneurship in sport due to the increased popularity of both the social and sport fields of study. As Randerson et al. (2016:39) state, "social entrepreneurship or corporate socially responsible activities respond to a need for social value creation." In the past there has been an emphasis on purely economic motives for sports organizations but this has changed with the increased emphasis on how to create value by encouraging collaboration with the community. Social value creation is included within many conceptualizations of corporate social responsibility as it provides a way for organizations to link with social issues An early definition of corporate social responsibility refers to it as "the obligations of businessmen to pursue those policies, to make those decisions, or to follow those lines of action which are desirable in terms of the objectives and values of our society" (Bowen, 1953:1). This seminal definition, whilst still used in the literature, has now shifted to a more entrepreneurial orientation due to the increased interest in social entrepreneurship.

In order for sports organizations to incorporate social entrepreneurship they need to have some imagination about future possibilities (Ratten and Jones, 2018). Entrepreneurial imagination is defined as "the ability to conceive of something seen only fragmentarily or superficially as a complete, perfected and integrated whole" (Chiles et al., 2010:10). The key premise of entrepreneurial imagination is in looking to the future and potential possibilities, which is crucial in the competitive sport global marketplace. This means the orientation of the imagination is the future rather than the past. This can be considered to be a process of imaginative visualization where opportunities not previously considered are appraised. This forward-thinking approach enables potential changes in the environment to be taken into account that enable new opportunities to emerge.

Barrett (2014:233) states "the concept of entrepreneurial imagination summarizes three broad imaginative concepts – empathy, modularity and self-organizing." Empathy involves thinking about other people's feelings and is important in seeing different points of view. In order to be a sport social entrepreneur it is helpful to have some empathy as it enables different thought processes to emerge (Miragaia et al., 2018). Modularity involves the various steps or tasks required in order to complete an action. Some tasks need to be done in a certain order whilst others can be completed in a flexible way. This is important for having a developmental process to incorporate social entrepreneurship in sports organizations. Self-organizing means doing things by oneself without direct orders or interaction. This can include having a sense of direction in terms of where an idea is heading and what is needed to achieve a goal. Athletes and other individuals involved in sports organizations can self-organize social enterprises as a way to engage in their passion for sport but also their interest in social entrepreneurship (Ratten, 2011).

There is a richness of topics within social entrepreneurship in sport that scholars need to pursue. As the global economy never stands still, the sports industry needs to take a dynamic approach to social entrepreneurship. As long as new technology is created the sports industry will continue to evolve. There are numerous questions about social entrepreneurship in sport that still lack a definitive answer and remain under-researched. For example, what determines the choice of sports organizations to become social entrepreneurs? How do institutions amplify the need for sport entities to be involved in social entrepreneurship? What are the cultural differences that discourage social entrepreneurship? Based on the potential answers to these questions there is a need for a more interdisciplinary approach to sport management that encompasses the health, social science and engineering disciplines (Ratten and Jones, 2018). This is due to there being different types of social entrepreneurship in sport but all have an underlying sense of social purpose.

Social entrepreneurship has been used in sport primarily as a way to impress community stakeholders rather than to attract new customers. More investment in social entrepreneurship practices is needed in the form of better workplace behaviors such as more information sharing. To convert social entrepreneurship into a competitive advantage there needs to be better group coordination and feedback mechanisms. This will enhance the perception of social entrepreneurship and factor in actionable ways to improve engagement. In order to craft a tangible strategic social entrepreneurship agenda there needs to be continuity between the social agenda and operational entrepreneurship practices. This will enable more effective group processes that can help measure the impact of social entrepreneurship (Ratten, 2017).

Sport management academics and practitioners have acknowledged a nascent shift in research to entrepreneurship. Sports organizations can augment social entrepreneurship by creating a favorable environment for it to flourish. This is important, as considerably more research is needed in order to further understand the relationship between sports organizations and social entrepreneurship. This book has attempted to identify the main characteristics of social entrepreneurship in sport through a review of the existing literature. The results enable the aggregation of the literature about social entrepreneurship in sport by focusing on its value in society and its embeddedness in communities.

Social entrepreneurship is an active topic for sports organizations and is gaining in popularity. Larger companies are fostering social entrepreneurship in sport by stepping up support for new programs and initiatives. New working models for social entrepreneurship in sport are being developed that will further establish its legitimacy (Ratten, 2016). Worldwide there has been more emphasis on including social entrepreneurship programs in sport as a way to bridge the profit/non-profit divide. Whilst the topic is practically important, there is a lack of theoretical development specifically applied to sport. This book will encourage more scholars to explicitly address social entrepreneurship in sport, thereby building a better understanding of the topic. The benefit for sports organizations of taking a social entrepreneurship perspective is that it pursues both social and financial objectives. This is important for sports organizations that need to focus on monetary gain whilst keeping good public relations. The literature on social entrepreneurship has tended to view all industries in the same manner without taking into account specific industry contexts. In the sports industry, there is a novel bridge between government and private involvement in firm activity. This results in government policies having social impact regulating sports club behavior. Sports organizations can be opportunistic when they deliver social value that has financial benefits. In particularly, social marketing of sport endeavors can use entrepreneurship as a way to think outside the box. The spirit of social entrepreneurship essentially involves developing new business ideas through a process of continual innovation. This process has been studied in a broad sense in general social entrepreneurship literature but not well understood in sport.

Progress on social entrepreneurship in sport

Whilst much progress on social entrepreneurship has been made, as demonstrated by the chapters in this book, there is still a need for a deeper understanding about its role in the sports industry. There are several promising areas for future research coming from the chapters of this book. Largely absent from the discussion of social entrepreneurship is the negative or opportunity costs arising from its practice. The literature would benefit from incorporating a more holistic perspective of social entrepreneurship in sport by including a multiplicity of approaches. This means including different stakeholder perspectives and discussing the way environments shape behavior. By taking into consideration the benefits and problems of social entrepreneurship, a better contextual understanding of the topic will emerge. Some of our knowledge about social entrepreneurship is taken for granted and there is a reluctance in researchers to challenge existing assumptions. Social entrepreneurship, like any form of entrepreneurship, can be studied in different ways.

This book will contribute to the further development of social entrepreneurship in the sport field. Although more support and guidance is needed on navigating research on this topic it would be helpful for future researchers to add to the conversation on social entrepreneurship in sport by providing more insight. To do this, researchers need to state how they contribute to the discussion whilst advancing the field of social entrepreneurship in sport. This requires perseverance but it is worthwhile considering the global and societal impact of social entrepreneurship. By dedicating research specifically to social entrepreneurship in sport, we will see some very interesting studies emerging from the literature.

This book highlights how researchers need to adopt a multidisciplinary approach to understanding social entrepreneurship in sport. The phenomenon of social entrepreneurship incorporates different levels including users, communities, businesses and government entities. Thus, to grasp how social entrepreneurship occurs in sport there needs to be a better consideration of the unique nuances of the sports industry. This helps to make a more meaningful contribution to the literature. By challenging the status quo in both sport and social entrepreneurship research more useful findings can emerge. This provides a better sense of where the literature is heading and what needs to be done to get there. The field of social entrepreneurship and sport is moving in a new direction so it is an exciting time for researchers in this area. Social entrepreneurship is perceived as an important contribution to societal and economic well-being.

There are broad differences in the types of social entrepreneurship emerging in sport. This reflects the dichotomy between low and high levels of entrepreneurship. Whilst there is an acknowledgment about the different forms and intensity of social entrepreneurship, more research needs to have new theoretical stances. This would allow for the future of social entrepreneurship in sport to bridge out from traditional entrepreneurship theory to take new paths.

Sport businesses are important in the development of regional economies and have a historical significance in communities. There are both positive and negative influencers that sport business can have on regional economies that are often the topic of debate. Sport business is associated with knowledge spillovers that facilitate further economic development in the form of urban planning or new venture creation. In addition, there are branding and marketing benefits associated with sport business that are linked to the emotional health of citizens. This is due to many people having an emotional attachment to sport via playing, watching or being involved in it in different ways.

Main contributions of the book

In this book I comprehensively reviewed how social entrepreneurship affects the sports industry. After reading this book the way that social entrepreneurship is an integral part of the sports industry should be clear. Social value creation has a significant impact on sport and helps increase its competitive advantage. Some of the most important factors affecting social entrepreneurship are leadership and knowledge-sharing behavior in sports organizations. To ensure more social entrepreneurship there needs to be an increase in the quality of information shared. This will increase the interaction amongst entities in a sport context.

The findings of this book need to be understood in light of the current economic and social climate. Sports organizations impact communities in a way that is different to other types of organizations. For sports organizations involved in social entrepreneurship there needs to be more effort in building social value creation. This can result in better community engagement that can filter through to other industry and business segments. More research is necessary to add to the findings of this book by utilizing diverse sport samples to better understand social entrepreneurship, although the generalizability of the findings of this book can be extended to other industry groups. The way in which social entrepreneurship is managed plays an important role in the ability of sports organizations to engage in community projects. Effective social entrepreneurship means building on the attitudes of sports organizations to illustrate how they can socially contribute to communities. This means having trust in social entrepreneurship activities and understanding how managers can contribute to better outcomes.

Practically speaking, social entrepreneurship is relevant for sport in general but there is no adequate set of guidelines to manage this process. Sports organizations do not convey the same social entrepreneurship outputs, as their success is an outcome of different environmental factors. There are risks associated with social entrepreneurship that can influence a sport firm's performance. This is due to sports organizations, which are engaging in social entrepreneurship, being major contributors to economic development, however it is hard to generalize all sports organizations due to their specific intricacies. Thus, there tend to be two contradictory perspectives about whether sports organizations are socially entrepreneurial. One perspective suggests that sports organizations, due to their social networks and embeddedness in society, are naturally producers and receivers of social causes. This reflects the view that sports organizations change based on the dynamism in the global business environment. The opposite view highlights the bureaucratic and sometimes corrupt nature of sports organizations that is orientated towards capitalism. In this view, sports organizations have changed to become big businesses that are only interested in financial gain. Both schools of thought about whether sports organizations are socially entrepreneurial, or not, have some merit.

Each of the chapters in this book contributes significantly to our understanding of social entrepreneurship in sport. Collectively the chapters represent a contribution to the nascent literature linking social entrepreneurship to sport. This book's main contributions are:

- an analytic overview of social entrepreneurship in sport
- a systematic review of different factors affecting social entrepreneurship
- suggested ways to incorporate more social entrepreneurship in sport

- how to meet the challenges that arise in implementing social change in sport
- guidelines for including more social entrepreneurship activity
- benefits of knowledge-sharing about social entrepreneurship
- future research suggestions and trends

Sports organizations are increasingly identifying themselves as engines for social entrepreneurship. As an activity, social entrepreneurship is becoming internalized into sports organizations. This is a defining feature of social entrepreneurship in sport. There is scant research on the potential link between social entrepreneurship and sport, which means there is a disconnect in the literature with new and emerging research areas. A contributing factor to this omission is the lack of literature that links social entrepreneurship to other research areas. In order to build the current research on sport and social entrepreneurship new lines of enquiry are needed. This will enable social enterprises that have exhibited greater levels of success to be studied in more detail. In high-growth sports organizations, social entrepreneurship has been used as a marketing tool.

As an important way to link social issues and sport, sport-based social entrepreneurship is the process of using social business ideas in a sport context. A considerable body of research recognizes the social importance of sports organizations in the global economy. Sports organizations are first and foremost leisure and health organizations but they also undertake considerable socially orientated activities. Sports organizations are part of an entrepreneurial ecosystem that needs to continually change to take new trends into account. However, there is an increasingly blurred boundary between the public and private activities of sports organizations, which requires further research.

Research streams

The discipline of social entrepreneurship is being enriched by the incorporation of sport examples. There are many examples of social entrepreneurship in the sports industry, including health intervention programs and multicultural engagement games but relatively little research has been conducted on these topics. The research questions this book has focused on include: How is social entrepreneurship different in a sport context? What trends can be observed in social entrepreneurship and sport? And how does social entrepreneurship in sport contribute to a more multidisciplinary research agenda?

The concept of social entrepreneurship in sport is undertheorized and lacks a cohesive theoretical foundation. It is unclear how sport social ventures differ from other social ventures and why the sports industry has a high concentration of social enterprises. Whilst it may seem obvious that sport, due to its role in the community, is naturally a place for social ventures there still needs to be a solid justification to back up these ideas. There seems to be a generalization of social entrepreneurship amongst all industries rather than rigorous attention to a sport context. This has meant the social entrepreneurship literature has remained static rather than capturing the dynamism of the sports industry. Thus, there has been little consideration of sport in terms of the networks of interactions that impact social entrepreneurship. There are specific people, places and processes that nurture sport social ventures. Some sports are more conducive to social entrepreneurship due to the attitudes of athletes or club members. Other sports might inhibit or refrain from social entrepreneurship due to a focus on profit maximization activities. However, once sports organizations start engaging in social entrepreneurship there are likely to be benefits both in terms of other entrepreneurial ventures and community sentiment.

The sports industry is an active contributor to the local economic and social dynamics of a region. There is a wide consensus that sport has an important role to play in the economy and is a core part of modern society. Sport management involves the planning and coordination of sport-related activities. The effective management of goods, services and related information about sport is needed as the importance of sport has changed over the last decade with more emphasis on broadcasting and Internet technology. In its early stages, sport was identified with leisure pursuits and considered more of an amateur activity. This has changed in recent times with sport becoming big business and linked to other industry sectors such as education and tourism. Originally sport was viewed as an independent area and it was researched predominantly by kinesiology and health science academics. Since sport has become more commercial it is now necessary to consider its impact on global competition. From a global perspective, sport management is now focused on information and knowledge rather than just physical activities. The activities involved in sport management range from clothing, products, forecasting, gambling and player coordination. In addition, there has been a rapid spread of online sport gambling, which has meant sport games are now played and viewed in different ways. Thus, the past silo approach to sport management is outdated and now needs to incorporate a more integrated system. This involves shifting the focus of sport from tangible assets (i.e., products) to intangible services (e.g., data analytics). The move generally to the knowledge economy is part of this trend and knowledge related to sport is valuable. In today's sport management environment, it is viewed as complex due to new knowledge being constantly acquired.

The potential for entrepreneurship stemming from sports organizations generating ideas seems to be largely unexploited in the literature. Support from organizations on the generation of ideas about social entrepreneurship is important to the sports industry but ideas about social entrepreneurship are less frequently implemented in sports organizations. With respect to the role of social entrepreneurship in sport, this book advances the finding that sport is a good arena for social practices. More work on exploring social entrepreneurship in sport is needed to understand the factors that impede the generation of new ideas. Sophisticated theoretical frameworks are required that suggest a social entrepreneurial stance in sports organizations.

The term "social entrepreneurship in sport" may be ambiguous to some, which implies a common definition is needed. Whilst previous studies have shown social entrepreneurship is viewed differently in sport, there is still a need for a clearer distinction. The understanding of social entrepreneurship might be viewed as being similar to other concepts such as corporate social responsibility but are in reality quite different. This implies that a distinct approach to managing social entrepreneurship is needed. I urge future researchers to expand their research to encompass social entrepreneurship in sport. This is crucial as the increased demands to be seen as innovative give rise to a need for sports organizations to focus on social entrepreneurship. This book has captured the essence of social entrepreneurship in sport but more research is needed.

Sport scholars have noted the importance of including entrepreneurship in research. This is derived from both sport and social entrepreneurship literature highlighting the need to take an interdisciplinary perspective to enlarge the scope of research. The purpose of social entrepreneurship in sport is open for conjecture due to the different social issues evident in sport. Table 7.1 below depicts some research themes on sport and social entrepreneurship that still need to be addressed in the literature. These themes are categorized in terms of firm, community, regional and international contexts for research.

Novel research directions

There is a need for novel directions in the area of social entrepreneurship in order to discover new opportunities. Social entrepreneurship in sport is a distinct area of study that involves recognizing opportunities that sports organizations can participate in. No matter what kind of social entrepreneurship is involved it starts with an opportunity. Some opportunities evolve into great ideas whilst others wither and die. This means the opportunity process starts with an individual or group of people then progresses, depending on resource availability. Opportunities can involve one individual or a firm that takes responsibility for the leadership of the project. In a sport context, opportunities present themselves in different ways depending on the intention and perceived success of the idea. There is a degree of risk in pursuing opportunities but this can be overcome through a risk/benefit analysis. To be sure, most social enterprises face risk but they manage this through careful interventions. Some social entrepreneurs will change their direction depending on whether their idea is suitable over the long term. Although initially ideas are new and novel, over time they become redundant. This means it is useful to ask social entrepreneurs their expected time frame for ideas and the reasons they are interested in a specific idea. Engaging with a social entrepreneur about their ideas will enable a better action process to evolve. This can include getting assistance from others to help them develop their idea and make it a reality in the marketplace.

The findings from this book can lay the groundwork for more large-scale quantitative studies on sport social entrepreneurs. There are unique dynamics of sport social entrepreneurs that need to be analyzed using large sample sizes that are collected over a number of different time periods. This would enable a longitudinal study to emerge that provides a comparison over time. The changes in

TABLE 7.1 Research themes for social entrepreneurship in sport

Context of research	Research questions
Firm level	How do sports organizations utilize social entrepreneurship?
	What is different about social entrepreneurship in sport compared to non-sports organizations?
	How do small, medium and large sports organizations differ in their use of social entrepreneurship?
	How do economic conditions affect the propensity of sports organizations to engage in social entrepreneurship?
	How are social enterprises created in a sport firm?
	Does the economic geography affect the amount of sports organizations involved in social entrepreneurship?
Community level	How do communities encourage sports organizations to use social entrepreneurship?
	Do existing networks help social enterprises develop in sport?
	What is the role of local government policy for encouraging sport-based social enterprises?
	What community factors and processes impact sport social enterprises?
	How do different types of community initiatives (e.g., fundraising) influence sport-based social enterprises?
Regional level	How do regional policies influence sport-based social entrepreneurship?
	To what extent does culture influence regions to use sport-based social entrepreneurship?
International level	How are international aid agencies using social entrepreneurship in a sport context?
	What is the role of culture in creating sport-related social enterprises?
	How do regional trading blocs influence sport-based social entrepreneurship?
	How do sports organizations that are engaged in social entrepreneurship contribute to regional economic development?

attitudes and behaviors of sport social enterprises are susceptible to environmental influencers. Therefore, an interesting avenue for future studies is to compare social entrepreneurs at different points in their journey. Other contextual factors such as geographic location and political conditions might influence the degree of social entrepreneurship occurring in a sport context.

Conclusion

This book should be of interest to a broad spectrum of people who practice, research and teach sport management and/or social entrepreneurship. The book explicates the interplay between sport and social entrepreneurship, which are underexplored concepts in the literature. Social entrepreneurship in sport presents an important but largely untapped research field. For those interested in promoting social entrepreneurship, sport provides a useful way to link theory to practice. This book highlights how the unique attributes of the sports industry continually reshape entrepreneurial activity. To respond to the changes in the global environment sports organizations need to orchestrate new entrepreneurial endeavors. A more entrepreneurial perspective to sport helps contribute to the market development of the industry. Entrepreneurship provides a way to explain the performance of the sports industry compared to its peers.

I began writing this book with an ambitious agenda of compiling a state of the art understanding into sport and social entrepreneurship research. Each of the chapters in this book focuses on different aspects of social entrepreneurship in a sport setting, thereby providing novel insights into social entrepreneurship and sport. I learnt a great deal whilst writing this book including how integral social value creation is in the sports industry. In addition, I learnt that whilst there has been a significant increase in general social entrepreneurship research we still do not know much about the topic in a sport setting. This has impeded the growth of the sport and social entrepreneurship field. However, I am observing more researchers interested in this topic, made evident by the practical significance of the field. This means sport and social entrepreneurship research can extend existing theories in order to take into account changing societal conditions. I conclude that sport and social entrepreneurship has the potential to be a popular sub-segment of business research. Therefore, the time is right for more scholars to focus on sport and social entrepreneurship as a way to raise the profile of the field.

References

Barrett, M. (2014) "Revisiting women's entrepreneurship: Insights from the family-firm context and radical subjectivist economics," *International Journal of Gender and Entrepreneurship*, 6(3): 231–254.

Bowen, H. R. (1953) *Social responsibilities of the businessman*. New York: Harper&Row.

Chiles, T., Tuggle, C., McMullen, J., Bierman, L. and Greening, D. (2010) "Dynamic creation: Extending the radical Austrian approach to entrepreneurship," *Organization Studies*, 31(1): 7–46.

Miragaia, D. A. M., da Costa, C. D. and Ratten, V. (2018) "Sport events at the community level: A pedagogical tool to improve skills for students and teachers," *Education+ Training*, 60(5): 431–442.

Randerson, K., Dossena, G. and Fayolle, A. (2016) "The future of family business: Family entrepreneurship," *Futures*, 75: 36–43.

Ratten, V. (2011) "Social entrepreneurship and innovation in sports," *International Journal of Social Entrepreneurship and Innovation*, 1(1): 42–54.

Ratten, V. (2016) "The dynamics of sport marketing: Suggestions for marketing intelligence and planning," *Marketing Intelligence & Planning*, 34(2): 162–168.

Ratten, V. (2017) *Sports innovation management*. London: Routledge.

Ratten, V. and Jones, P. (2018) "Sport education: Fit for a purpose," *Education+ Training*, 60(5): 370–374.

INDEX

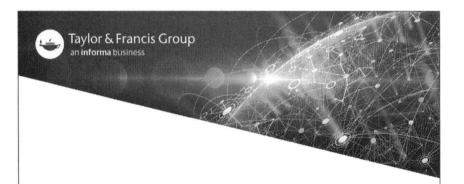

Printed in Great Britain
by Amazon